Organise Yourself

THE SUNDAY TIMES

Organise Yourself

John Caunt | Third Edition

KoganPage

LONDON PHILADELPHIA NEW DELHI

Publisher's note
Every possible effort has been made to ensure that the information contained in
this book is accurate at the time of going to press, and the publishers and authors
cannot accept responsibility for any errors or omissions, however caused. No
responsibility for loss or damage occasioned to any person acting, or refraining
from action, as a result of the material in this publication can be accepted by the
editor, the publisher or the author.

First published 2000
Second edition 2006
Third edition 2010

120 Pentonville Road	525 South 4th Street, #241	4737/23 Ansari Road
London N1 9JN	Philadelphia PA 19147	Daryaganj
United Kingdom	USA	New Delhi 110002
www.koganpage.com		India

© John Caunt, 2000, 2006, 2010

The right of John Caunt to be identified as the author of this work has been
asserted by him in accordance with the Copyright, Designs and Patents Act 1988.

ISBN   978 0 7494 5583 5
E-ISBN   978 0 7494 5909 3

The views expressed in this book are those of the author, and are not necessarily
the same as those of Times Newspapers Ltd.

British Library Cataloguing in Publication Data

A CIP record for this book is available from the British Library.

Library of Congress Cataloging-in-Publication Data

Caunt, John.
    Organise yourself / John Caunt. -- 3rd ed.
       p. cm.
    ISBN 978-0-7494-5583-5 -- ISBN 978-0-7494-5909-3 (e-bk) 1. Time management.
2. Personal information management. 3. Life skills. I. Title.
    HD69.T54C39 2010
    650.1'1--dc22   2009043348

Typeset by Jean Cussons Typesetting, Diss, Norfolk
Printed and bound in India by Replika Press Pvt Ltd

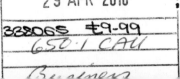

Contents

Introduction

Never have we experienced a greater need to be organised.

The working environment of today is characterised by constantly rising pressure to deliver with fewer resources. Against a background of restructuring and cost-cutting we are expected to keep a larger number of balls in the air and to do so with less support. The picture is increasingly one of self-sufficient professionals responsible for all aspects of their workplace organisation. The information age provides us with some of the tools to organise our working lives, but it also presents us with many new challenges in the form of increased volumes of information, constant connectedness, expectations of immediacy, and interruptions to our routines.

Outside our working lives, we have greater expectations of our leisure time, and we readily expect to be able to fulfil family commitments while we and our partners hold down demanding jobs. We juggle the different elements of our lives to cram in trips and excursions, duty visits, entertainment, house-keeping, health pursuits, personal development, voluntary responsibilities, family activities and time with friends.

To cope with all of this we need to be organised. We need to handle time, information, people and technology as efficiently and effectively as possible in order to deliver the results on which we will be judged. Being organised means:

- **less time spent firefighting and responding to crises;**
- **sharper focus on the things that matter most in terms of producing results;**
- **the ability to see your way through complex problems and challenges;**
- **more time for family, friends and leisure;**
- **reduced stress and fatigue;**
- **greater sense of achievement;**
- **the chance to step back and take pride in a job well done.**

Even though the benefits of greater organisation are clear, we present ourselves with excuses for failing to acquire them:

Excuse 1 – 'The ability to be organised is something innate. It's a quality that you either possess or lack, and I just don't have it.'

Certainly it's true that we vary in our natural tendency towards being organised, but it isn't true that there is nothing we can do to overcome that inclination. Studies of brain function have revealed differences in the way that the two hemispheres of the brain operate. Work by American psychologist Jerre Levy and others demonstrated that the left hemisphere is superior in analytical functioning, while the right hemisphere is superior in many forms of visual and spatial performance and tends to be more holistic in its functioning than the left. It has been shown that although we use both hemispheres of the brain simultaneously, there is a tendency in most of us to favour one side or the other. We are either left-brain dominant or right-brain dominant. In simple terms, the left-brain dominant person tends towards an organised, analytical and methodical approach, while right-brain dominant types tend to be more creative and intuitive. However, just because we may favour one way of operating, it does not mean that we are unable to develop the skills associated with the other hemisphere. In truth, we all display skills associated with both sides of the brain. When it comes to organising skills, the right-brain dominant person may just have to work a bit harder at it than the left-brain dominant individual. And just in case you are wondering, I'll own up now to being a person who has to work quite hard at being organised.

> Excuse 2 – 'There is no way that I could be organised in this place. The constant interruptions, the crises, the disorganised colleagues.'

Yes, there are plenty of workplaces where it is hard to be organised, but that is no reason to give up. In the chapters that follow we will look at how you can take control of your working environment and reduce interruptions and distractions. We will look at the effect of good planning in forestalling crises, effective delegation which minimises colleague dependency, and ways of helping others to be more organised.

> Excuse 3 – 'I would like to be more organised but I'm just too busy to spend time on it at the moment. Perhaps in a couple of months' time.'

In today's work climate, the person who postpones action in the hope of having more time a month, two months, six months from now, is destined to be forever disappointed. And what does 'being too busy' really mean? It is possible to spend your working days scurrying in every direction and achieving little – you may be busy but not effective. Targeted activity is what brings results, and improved organisation is largely about targeting your activity.

For many of us the aim of getting organised has a great deal in common with those other ubiquitous lifestyle objectives – getting fit or losing weight. We believe it will be good for us and our lives will be fuller and more satisfying if we can accomplish it, but somehow we never seem to achieve it to the degree or with the consistency we seek. In the same way as we embark on successive diets and fitness programmes, so we pitch ourselves into organisational splurges that may bear fruit for a while before we sink back into our depressingly chaotic old ways. We latch onto some new regime or rush to acquire the piece of equipment or software that we believe will solve our organisational problems for us. And perhaps, for a time, it seems to do the trick. But then we lose our focus, the old habits start to reappear, systems go down the tubes and procrastination is the order of the day.

It doesn't have to be like that. Everyone can become more organised – and not just for a month or three months, but permanently. However, there's no instant fix – sustainable change requires more than a new gadget or a few quick tips. It requires attention to your current attitudes and expectations, a degree of perseverance in building new routines, and readiness to pull together all the threads – time, information, people and technology – to produce a package of actions that will work for you.

So, if you have made previous attempts at better organisation that haven't worked out, don't despair. You can do it, and I hope this book will provide you with many of the strategies needed to get you there. But don't adopt everything I suggest religiously: be prepared to adapt or experiment with what is written here and build a system that is not mine, but yours.

Whilst most of the examples used in this book are work related, the principles and strategies suggested are just as applicable to those seeking to bring better organisation into their home, leisure or voluntary activity. Nor, from a work point of view, should it be assumed that there is any perceived target audience in terms of occupational groups or levels of workforce seniority. The pressures of the modern workplace are fairly universal, and the steps to improved personal organisation are pretty much the same whatever your job. There will be differences, of course, in the volumes and nature of information you are required to handle, the amount of support you are able to call upon and the number of colleagues, clients and contacts you have to relate to. But whether you are a newly appointed junior, an established professional or a self-employed home worker, there is something here for you.

In those sections that deal with aspects of technology, it is assumed that most readers will have some awareness of computers but that their knowledge may be piecemeal. Where specific techniques are referred to, I have used as examples the most popular applications at the time of writing. This applies particularly to the Microsoft Windows operating system and Office software. Users of other applications and operating systems may need to refer to their software documentation or help file.

1

Know where you are going

This book contains information on a whole range of techniques, technology and tips to assist with your personal organisation, but none will do the trick without the first essential ingredient. That is you and your approach to the process of becoming more organised. The first step to being organised occurs not in your inbox, your filing cabinet or your computer, but in your head. If you are to take control of your life and begin to make a difference, you must address your organisational weaknesses and strengths, the reasons for current disorganisation and your attitude towards changing the situation. You should ensure too that you have a clear idea of where you are heading and how you expect to get there.

We all have our organisational strengths and weaknesses, so before going any further take a moment to ask yourself where your particular shortcomings lie. Which of the following statements apply to you?

- **There is a lack of overall direction to my work.**
- **I have difficulty extracting priorities from the mass of tasks and issues that come my way.**

- My days seem to slip away with little achieved.
- I don't plan my time adequately.
- I end the day with more items on my 'to do' list than I started with.
- I find it hard to estimate how long some tasks are going to take.
- Deadlines seem to creep up on me.
- I'm not sure that I make best use of the times when my energy levels are highest.
- I flit in and out of routine tasks, often letting them interrupt more important work.
- I tend to postpone tasks I don't like.
- Trivial tasks assume greater importance than they should.
- I sometimes have difficulty knowing where to start on complex tasks and projects.
- I would like to be more systematic in my decision making.
- The volume of incoming correspondence is a problem for me.
- I don't often tackle messages and documents when I first look at them.
- I am often unable to decide what to do with information I receive.
- I would like to assimilate documents more quickly.
- I forget a lot of what I read.
- I find myself attending too many unproductive meetings.
- I don't think I delegate enough.
- Colleagues bombard me with information I don't need.
- I am plagued by interruptions.
- Too often I take on tasks I should refuse.
- My workspace layout isn't conducive to good organisation.
- There are piles of paper in my office, my desktop is cluttered and cupboards and drawers are crammed.
- I spend a lot of time looking for things.

- My files are disorganised.
- I am concerned that I am not adequately utilising technology to organise my work.
- I don't use the internet as effectively as I might.
- My personal organisation declines when I am working from home or away from the office.

Reasons for disorganisation

The above checklist aims to help you identify some of your current organisational weaknesses, but it's useful also to explore the reasons for them. In broad terms we could say there are three main drivers of disorganisation: external pressures, systems failures and personal factors. The first includes such things as overload, interruptions, and problems with the working environment, while the second relates to absence of strategies and routines for managing time and information, and failure to use tools appropriately. It is the third area that we most often neglect. Personal factors affecting disorganisation might include anxiety about certain tasks or a desire for novelty that leads us to flit from one task to another. Also present might be a tendency towards perfectionism, a habit of taking on too much, an unwillingness to delegate or a failure to say no on occasions. All of these problems can be tackled, but first they need to be recognised, so take a moment now to ask yourself this question: 'What are the main reasons why I am currently less organised than I would wish to be?' Jot down your responses. They will be useful in an objective-setting activity later in the chapter.

Attitudes towards organising

Disorganisation is not, in the main, something about which we feel a sense of shame. In fact we can present it to ourselves as almost an endearing quality – an indication that there is more to us than boring routines, rigid attention to maintaining schedules or an obsessive desire to ensure that everything is in its proper place. As long as we persist in such attitudes, we are likely to hold some inner resistance to becoming more organised, and the changes we seek will be more difficult.

In the Introduction I presented some of the excuses we give ourselves for not becoming more organised, but sometimes there are more than just excuses. We may have entrenched beliefs about ourselves that hold us back even when we have decided to act. Beliefs such as these can lead us to doubt our ability to change:

- **'I've been like this so long I'm not sure I can change my ways.'**
- **'I'm just naturally untidy.'**
- **'I'm so easily distracted – can't keep my attention on anything for long.'**

One way to shift such unhelpful beliefs is to search out contrary evidence. Take a good look at your life and the likelihood is you will be able to find areas where you are organised. Perhaps good organisation is apparent in some leisure interest to which you are able to give time and attention despite your otherwise busy schedule. Maybe it occurs in aspects of your domestic arrangements. Even in areas of your life where chaos appears to rule, there will be pockets of good organisation – items that are stored where you are always able to put your hands on them and routines that get the job done quickly and effectively. What is it about these aspects of your work or your life that has made them different? Are there features of your organisational successes that you can transfer into other elements of your life? Focus on the things that are working well in addition to those that are not, and use them to build a more positive view of the way forward. Have a go now at listing your organisational strengths – the things that are working well for you, in whatever area of your life they are to be found. Writing them down will generally add to the value of the exercise.

If you are to remove unhelpful attitudes towards organisation, it is also important to weed out any negative self-talk. Statements like 'I'm never able to muscle down to tasks', whether made privately to yourself or shared in conversation with others, only serve to reinforce a sense of helplessness. Replace them with positive affirmations – simple strong statements repeated regularly to yourself: 'I can achieve everything I set out to do.' 'I can handle interruptions and get back on track.' 'I can change disorganised habits.' 'I can cope with whatever the day throws at me.' Choose some affirmations that are right for you and mentally repeat these statements of faith in yourself on a regular basis.

It's essential too that you shift any attitudes that may reinforce the notion that organisation is a wholly tedious process or that disorganised people are somehow more interesting than their more organised colleagues. Visualise the benefits of a better-organised lifestyle. How will it feel? What will better organisation offer you that you don't have at present?

Visualising the benefits of greater organisation is made easier if you have a clear view of what your objectives actually are, but in a busy, multifaceted life this may be more easily said than done. You may have a host of vaguely articulated goals, commitments and aspirations. Some will overlap; some may conflict. There will be those that you have originated and others over which you have little control. They may be associated with any of the elements that constitute your life: work, leisure activities, family and relationships, voluntary responsibilities, learning and development.

At a later stage in the process of becoming more organised it may be useful for you to spend some time shaping up a coherent set of life objectives, but for now let me ask a simple question that, in the context of this book, helps to identify some of the things that are important to you.

Why do you want to be more organised?

Ask yourself that question now. Jot down all the answers that come to mind and follow any trail that an answer generates.

Example

Q. Why do I want to be more organised?

A. So that I don't have to work so many hours.

Q. How would I wish to use the time saved through greater organisation?

A. Getting fit; learning Spanish; spending more time with the people I care about.

Q. Why do I want to get fit?

A. Ability to take part in a range of outdoor activity, greater confidence and self-respect.

Q. Why do I want to be more organised?

A. To show that I'm on top of my job.

Q. Why do I want to show that I'm on top of my job?

A. To demonstrate that I'm worthy of promotion.

Q. Why do I want to be more organised?

A. To gain a greater sense of satisfaction from the projects I undertake.

Q. Why am I seeking that greater sense of satisfaction?

A. Because all my activities currently feel like chaotic drudgery. It doesn't have to be like that.

Pursuing this question helps to shift the sort of negative attitudes I was referring to earlier and reinforces the point that the changes you are seeking are not ends in themselves, but means to achieving those things that are really important in your work and your life in general.

An understanding of broad aims is an important starting point to becoming more organised. But the next essential step is to identify the practical things that will have to be accomplished if you are to achieve those aims, and that means giving some attention to setting objectives. Let's take a look at objective setting now.

Setting objectives

Whether you are thinking about major life goals, the requirements of a work project or the process of becoming more organised, time spent determining your objectives is more than likely to be repaid. Unfortunately, objective setting is often hedged around with a certain amount of jargon and mystique that can deter the uninitiated. But it doesn't have to be a big deal. An objective is just a tool, the purpose of which is to transform amorphous challenges into tasks you can get your teeth into and that will lead to meaningful outcomes. It needs to be clear and precise, but don't go overboard in your search for complete precision. An objective that is a little loose is better than no objective at all. This is particularly the case when you are setting objectives for yourself rather than for others. You know what you mean; others might not.

Try to produce objectives that are SMART – specific, measurable, achievable, results oriented and time related.

Specific

The more general an objective, the harder it is to focus on those tasks and activities necessary to bring about its achievement. As an example let's consider your purpose in reading this book. You're doing it because you want to become more organised. That's OK as a general aim but it's not much help in getting to where you want to be. For that, you need to break your general aim down into objectives that are more specific in terms of the things you are going to do. The specifics are those things you may already have identified as weaknesses to be resolved – for example, overcoming procrastination, clarifying priorities or eliminating clutter.

Measurable

Without a measurable element to your objectives you have no way of determining at what point they have been achieved, and the resultant vagueness may mean a loss of focus. You might decide, for example, that one of your objectives in respect of personal organisation is to improve your typing speed. But what constitutes successful achievement – an improvement of one word per minute, or an improvement of 30? Only with some idea of scale does the objective have precision. And don't neglect the fact that there may need to be more than one measurable element if an objective is to have any value. An increase in typing speed of 30 words a minute may be entirely achievable but at a cost to accuracy that renders the improvement meaningless. Whilst you may be prepared to sacrifice some degree of accuracy in the initial drive towards increasing performance, you will want to ensure that such losses are recovered later on. However, don't be too rigid or arbitrary in the measurable elements you introduce to your objectives. Excessive quantification may actually hamper achievement as attention spent on measuring gets in the way of what is being measured. And lack of flexibility may mean that you hit a brick wall when unforeseen obstacles appear, or may even lead you to ignore opportunities for further development beyond the stated target.

Achievable

Any objective you set should be achievable. The reason you are using the objective is in order to get things done and to obtain the positive reinforcement that comes from success. It is not the purpose of objectives to add unnecessary stress to your life and deliver the negative reinforcement of failure. On the other hand, there is little to be gained by setting objectives that can be achieved with minimal effort. You may get a slight buzz when you cross them off your list of things to do, but deep down you won't be fooled by the illusion of progress. The trick is to set immediate objectives that are just out of reach. It's a matter of having to stretch yourself to achieve them, but not to saddle yourself with aspirations that will be impossible to meet.

Does that mean that you can't have a grand objective – a target that is well beyond your current capabilities? No, it doesn't, provided that you break down your main objectives into sub-goals and work towards your grand vision in manageable steps.

You might, for example, have a grand objective of reducing the weekly hours you spend on work matters from a current average of 55 to an average of 40, while maintaining current levels of output and quality. This is most probably a target that will require attention to many of the elements covered in this book, and should be broken down into sub-goals, each with realistic stages towards achievement. One such sub-goal might concern improved ability to delegate. But within this there needs to be recognition that the early stages of such a process might actually mean an investment of more time, as you give attention to such activities as identifying those tasks it is possible to delegate, briefing the people who will take them on and working to ensure that the tasks are perceived as valuable and challenging. Your staged objectives should take account of this time investment and provide the space for it before the time savings start to kick in.

Results oriented

Objectives should be described in terms of results delivered rather than activities. If, as part of a drive to become more organised, you determine that you will arrive at work an hour earlier in the mornings, this simply describes the activity. You can spend that hour drinking coffee and chatting, and you will still meet the objective. A far better objective would include identification of those things you propose to achieve in the hour – possibly the completion of tasks that require uninterrupted concentration and are therefore more difficult to accomplish in the hurly-burly of the regular working day.

Time related

Objectives generally benefit from clear deadlines by which they will be completed. This links closely with the requirement that they be achievable. An objective may be achievable in one timescale but not in another. Deadlines are also helpful in providing motivation and maintaining momentum, provided that they are related to a period of time that you are able to get hold of. A deadline six months hence is too vague and distant for most of us. If we are to maintain consistent effort and motivation for a period of more than a month, then we will generally benefit from breaking our target down into smaller stages – individual weeks or months. This may mean building in monthly milestones – review points on the road to your main goal – or setting a series of sub-goals. If, for example, you conclude that it should be possible over a period of three months to reduce the amount of time you spend in meetings from a current average of 12 hours a week to 6, you might set staged targets of a two hour per week reduction in each month with a specific monthly focus:

- **Month 1 – extricate yourself from unnecessary meetings.**
- **Month 2 – find more time-efficient alternative ways of doing some of the business currently conducted in meetings.**
- **Month 3 – improve the efficiency of those meetings you remain involved with.**

Activity

What are your objectives in terms of better organisa-tion? You gave some thought earlier in the chapter to why you want to be more organised, but it's time to get more specific. In the light of your responses to the checklist of current weaknesses, your analysis of the reasons why you are not as well organised as you might be and your answers to the question 'Why do you want to be more organised?', have a go now at articulating your main goals in respect of better organisation. Write them down, taking account of the above SMART points. In some cases, you might already have ideas of sub-goals and the detailed steps you expect to take towards the achievement of your main goal; if so, note these too. But don't be too concerned about producing a detailed action plan at this stage. There is a lot you already know about organisation and your own needs, and clarifying your thoughts at this stage will assist your assimilation and application of new ideas and techniques, but you will also have the opportunity to refine your views as you go through the book, and we will review progress and plan the way forward in the final chapter.

Balancing the different elements of your life

Your life is made up of a whole variety of elements each competing for your time and attention, and it's easy to be side-tracked into one element to the detriment of others. A particular activity may start to take up more of your attention than anticipated, or an interesting issue may draw you away from other priorities. Take care to focus on the big picture and apportion your limited resources in a balanced way to ensure that you make progress towards all your objectives.

Whatever your job or lifestyle, there is likely to be a range of conflicting demands upon your time. So spend a few moments now considering adjustments you might make to the activities that take up your time and energy.

Ask yourself:

1. Are there elements of my life that are currently taking a greater proportion of my time and attention than they should? If so, what are they?
2. Why have they become excessively demanding?
3. What elements of my life should I be spending more time on?
4. What might I do to start adjusting the balance between these?

Try to formulate your answers to point 4 in terms of realistic objectives rather than vague intentions.

Determining day-to-day priorities

Life would be easy if, having planned the way forward, we could quietly and systematically pursue the achievement of our objectives. But it's seldom like that. In all probability, your day is spent responding to a multitude of routine chores, crises, requests and interruptions. In the face of this bombardment you need a means of determining which tasks will take priority. A simple way of looking at this is to define every demand upon your time, whether it is self-generated or comes in the form of a request, in terms of its importance and its urgency.

Any task can be slotted into one of the four sectors in Figure 1.1.

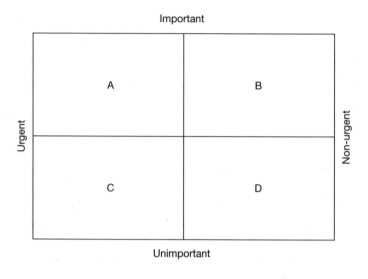

Figure 1.1   Determining priorities

Sector A: tasks that are important and urgent

Items that are both important and urgent are clearly the ones to
which you must give the most immediate attention, but they are
not always instantly identifiable. What constitutes 'important'
can be problematic. A manipulative colleague may persuade you
that what is important for him or her should feature just as
highly on your agenda. Even worse, you may be the guilty party
– convincing yourself that a minor diversion is an essential task
that simply cannot wait. 'Important' in this context should mean
important for the realisation of your main objectives – not just
those associated with your work, but wider, quality-of-life
objectives too. If a balanced lifestyle and family time have a high
priority for you, then getting to your child's first Christmas
concert will rightly be just as important as anything your
workplace can throw at you.

It's also worth questioning the notion of urgency. Once again it could be a case of other people's agendas rather than your own. It might be a matter of urgency that could have been avoided if you had planned your time better or if you had got down to work earlier rather than procrastinating. Some of us do our best work when spurred on by a sense of urgency, but urgency that you control – where you have set your own deadline or planned to work under time pressure – is a different matter from the sense of crisis and panic that comes from urgency that has crept up on you.

Sector B: tasks that are important but not urgent

Tasks in this sector generally present the biggest problems for those of us whose organisation is not as good as it could be. They tend to be concerned with longer-term objectives or major life-quality issues and we need to ensure that we find the time to progress them. But often we are guilty of ignoring or postponing them, allowing other less important but superficially more urgent or attractive activities to take their place. Given inadequate attention, category B tasks may suddenly be promoted to extreme category A when a deadline looms or, in the absence of any meaningful deadline, may simply not get done. Such is the fate of many life objectives that are actually very important to us but are endlessly postponed until they wither and die. Plan your time effectively to reduce this possibility, and try to ensure that as much of your time as possible is spent on category B tasks.

Sector C: tasks that are urgent but unimportant

Don't let these items draw your attention away from those in group B. Just because they are urgent doesn't make them any more important. Question why they are urgent. Often you will find it is no more than a gloss applied by others to justify their existence or cover their inefficiency. Such tasks may be ones to delegate or to run quietly into the sand. Of course, your decision on what to do about them may require an element of diplomacy. If your boss is the one asking, and he or she regards a particular task as important and urgent, then some adjustment of your own assessment may be necessary.

Sector D: tasks that are neither important nor urgent

You should not be wasting your time and energy on these. Frequently tasks in this category are used as self-generated distractions – excuses for not getting down to other more important work that for one reason or another we view with some degree of apprehension. Recognise them for what they are and focus your efforts on tasks in the other sectors.

The 80:20 rule
The 80:20 rule was originated by an Italian economist – Vilfredo Pareto – around 1900. He discovered a consistent phenomenon that about 80 per cent of the wealth of countries was controlled by around 20 per cent of the people. This 80:20 principle has since been expanded to include all aspects of business and management – notably '80 per cent of the results come from 20 per cent of the effort'. The accuracy of this relationship may be disputed, but the fact remains that, by concentrating your effort into the important few actions rather than the trivial many, you are liable to achieve more impressive results.

Summary

The first steps towards better organisation consist of:

- clarifying your current organisational strengths and weaknesses;
- identifying the reasons why you are currently not as organised as you might wish;
- building a positive belief in your ability to make progress;
- establishing a clear view of what you expect to gain from better organisation;
- setting precise objectives;
- balancing the different elements of your life;
- determining day-to-day priorities.

2

Organise your time

Time is unlike most other resources in that it is shared out equally. We all have the same amount of it each day. The differences between us lie in how we choose to spend it and how far we try to stretch it.

Your aim in managing your time better is either to reduce the number of hours you spend working, or to achieve more in the same number of hours. It is a matter of ordering priorities. When you say, 'I just haven't got the time for this', you are really saying, 'Something else is more important to me than this'. The problem is that, through inadequate planning and monitoring, we lose control of our schedule and fail to distinguish between the high pay-off and low pay-off demands on our time. We find ourselves saying, 'I haven't time for this' to an important commitment because we have already spent too much of it on trivia.

In this chapter, then, we will look at techniques for planning and tracking the tasks that we need to spend time on. First, however, let's consider how you currently spend your time.

How you use time now

It is useful, before embarking on a new planning regime for your time, to give some attention to how you are currently spending it. Some time management programmes propose that you maintain a rigid time log for a couple of weeks. I don't see this as necessary, but I do suggest that you carry out a simple monitoring exercise over a period of several days.

Monitoring exercise – task importance

The purpose of this exercise is to heighten your awareness of the relative importance of the tasks which go to make up your day, and to signal those areas on which you may concentrate your efforts for improvement. On a blank sheet of A4, recreate the diagram we encountered in Chapter 1, and label the four sectors as shown in Figure 2.1.

A. Important and urgent	B. Important, not urgent
C. Urgent, not important	D. Neither urgent nor important

Figure 2.1   Monitoring your tasks

Keep the sheet to hand throughout your working day and note the tasks you carry out in the appropriate sector as indicated in the example in Figure 2.2.

A. Important and urgent	B. Important, not urgent
Finished presentation for tomorrow's board meeting. Implemented emergency payment arrangements following payroll computer crash	Produced plan for office relocation. Reviewed progress with team. Investigated possible new business lead.
C. Urgent, not important	D. Neither urgent nor important
Responded to interruptions. Wrote replies to routine correspondence which could have been delegated.	Sat for 2 hours in irrelevant meeting I could have avoided. Browsed junk mail. Found some minor tasks to avoid less pleasant work.

Figure 2.2   Examples of priorities

Complete a sheet each day for a minimum of three days and compare them, asking yourself the following questions:

- Did I have any difficulty in distinguishing between those tasks that are important and those that are unimportant? If so, what steps do I need to take to remove this confusion?
- Roughly what proportion of my time is currently being spent on unimportant tasks? (Sectors C and D)
- What could I do to reduce the number of tasks appearing in these sectors?
- Was enough of my time spent on tasks in Sector B?
- How can I increase time devoted to these tasks?

If, in the course of this exercise, you find yourself discarding or delegating tasks you would normally have carried out, that's fine. It's the start of organising your time better. As an alternative to completing the sheets as you work, you may prefer to fill them in retrospectively, looking back over what you have done in the last week.

Planning and tracking your time

Having examined how your time is currently being spent, the next step is to adopt a workable system for planning and tracking your time through the days, weeks and months ahead.

Planning

You need to be able to:

- determine your objectives;
- identify the steps needed to achieve your objectives;
- break projects and assignments down into their component tasks;
- decide how long you expect activities to take;
- decide when you will need to complete tasks over the coming days and weeks;
- identify what you will need from others in order that you can complete your own tasks.

Tracking

You need to be able to keep track of:

- your contacts;
- your meetings and appointments;
- what you have done and what remains to be done;
- who is doing what for you and by when;
- when you should follow up contacts and leads.

Planning your time

Effective planning requires that you take account of different time frames. The relative importance of longer-term and short-term planning will vary according to the nature of your work, but you may like to look at planning over three time frames. The first, and most general, might be an overall view of the next three months in terms of major objectives; the second, a week-by-week view to be sure that you are able to fit in the necessary preparation for impending commitments and deadlines; and the third, a detailed daily plan to ensure that you achieve a balance between important and urgent items and tasks which contribute towards longer-term objectives.

Planning your day

The time to plan your day is not first thing in the morning, but at the end of the previous working day. Once you get into the habit it will take no more than a few minutes before you pack up for the day. The task is completed while your brain is still in work mode and the following morning you are spared any indecisiveness and time-wasting while you gear yourself up for the day. You know exactly what you are aiming to do and you are able to hit the ground running. Resist the temptation to be overambitious in the number of tasks you set yourself, and don't book yourself up so heavily that there is no space for the unexpected. Crossing completed items off your list is very satisfying and helps to keep you on track, but resist the temptation to include too many easy hits on your list – small tasks which are there simply to be crossed off.

Mapping out your week

Just like daily planning, the time to map out your week is at the end of the previous week. You're not concerned with the same level of detail as for the daily plan, but you are aiming to establish an overall balance to your week, and to ensure that you are not caught on the hop. You will be thinking about what information you need to ask for on Monday in order that it is available for a task that must be completed by Friday; what you will have to do on Tuesday to prepare for that meeting on Wednesday; how much you will need to do each day to carry forward a major long-term initiative.

A regular Friday afternoon session when you map out the coming week is also a good time to review your work in the current week and give yourself credit for the things you have achieved. Don't succumb to frustration about the tasks you have not managed to complete. Use the session as an opportunity to ask yourself why they haven't been completed:

- **Was there over-optimism on your part with respect to the number of tasks you allocated for the week?**
- **Did other important and unexpected work crop up that pushed some allocated tasks aside?**
- **Did something occur that made the tasks no longer necessary?**
- **Were you perhaps guilty of procrastination or avoidance?**

Consider whether the tasks concerned need to be rescheduled and, if so, slot them into your upcoming plan using, as appropriate, techniques suggested later in this chapter to ensure they are achieved.

Overviewing the next three months

This is at a different level again from your weekly planning. It's about major blocks of time that will need to be devoted to projects and development tasks. The aim here is to ensure that deadlines in respect of different assignments don't clash, and that the timescales you allocate to major tasks are realistic. You are most likely to engage in this sort of activity in conjunction with planning a particular project.

If you are not currently in the habit of systematically planning your time, or your previous efforts to do so have been unsuccessful, I suggest you go for a weekly overview initially, in conjunction with a master list of 'to do' items (see later section in this chapter). Once you have a system of weekly time planning up and running successfully, move on to more detailed planning of each day and an increased awareness of the longer-term dimension.

Tracking your time

Tracking is about keeping on top of the activities you have planned – ensuring that you are reminded when actions are due, and monitoring your progress towards achievement of the objectives you have set yourself. The key to this is simplicity. Wherever possible, avoid recording information in multiple locations. This is an issue particularly if you are using paper-based means of recording commitments. Using a desk diary in the office and a pocket diary when you are at meetings and on the road is a recipe for overlooked appointments. If it is essential to have information in different formats, make sure that there is one master record. Limit the amount of manual transfer of information as far as possible to avoid oversights and minimize wasted effort.

Planning and tracking tools

The tools you use to assist planning and tracking may range from a notebook and diary to a palmtop computer. Choose those that best suit your preferred style and the nature of your work. Remember, too, that a poorly used tool can impede rather than enhance your effectiveness.

It may be that your needs are adequately served at the simple end of the range – a notebook to record tasks and general reminders, and a diary for appointments and timed commitments. All other tools are variations on this basic format, and increased sophistication does not always mean greater effectiveness. However, those of us with large numbers of contacts, tasks and appointments will want a more advanced means of tracking them. Let's look at the merits of paper-based and electronic systems.

Paper-based planners and organisers

Back in the 1980s no self-respecting professional would be seen without a leather-bound personal organiser, and a visit to an office stationery supplier today will reveal that while numbers and ranges have declined, there are still plenty around, produced in a variety of styles and prices. The basic format is a small ring binder with indexed sections containing pre-printed insert pages. Typical inserts available include:

- **year planners;**
- **diaries in various formats;**
- **daily planning sheets – appointments and things to do;**
- **monthly objectives and project planning sheets;**
- **telephone and address book inserts;**
- **pages for notes;**
- **budget planning and expenses planning.**

The idea is that all necessary working information is contained in one convenient folder. Users can switch their attention easily from a long-term to a short-term view and can swiftly update information wherever they might be. New pages can be inserted and redundant ones removed so that the organiser remains indefinitely expandable and always up to date. The downside is that there may be some need to transfer information from one page to another and some of the tools, year planners for example, are a little too small for serious use. Also, if you have a large number of contacts for your address book or need to make a lot of notes, you can find these sections becoming unwieldy.

PC-based personal information managers (PIMs)

These are in effect customised databases for storing and tracking personal information. The main commercial packages also serve as e-mail clients. The most widely used is Outlook, which comes packaged with some versions of Microsoft Office, but there are numerous other good examples that can be downloaded from the internet, some free of charge. There are also online organisers, which generally operate on a subscription basis, although there are some free services at the simple end of the range. They have the advantage of being accessible from anywhere, and allow you to give others access to your diary outside the confines of your own network.

Typical contents of a personal information manager are:

- an address book to manage contacts;
- 'to do' lists which can be arranged under subject categories and may permit some simple project planning and tracking in terms of target date, person responsible, planned duration and percentage of the task completed;
- a calendar and appointments scheduler, which may be integrated with the address book and 'to do' lists, and which offers facilities for reminders and recurring appointments;
- recording of time spent on activities and expenses tracking;
- free note space which may be adapted to particular purposes.

The great benefit of a PIM is the way that information can be integrated and viewed in different ways, without the hassle of manually transferring it. You can plan your activities within a project, and slot tasks into your schedule over a period of weeks taking full account of your other commitments. On the appointed date for commencement of a task, the 'to dos' will pop up and won't go away until you have signalled them as complete. Regularly recurring commitments only need to be entered once. You can view the big picture and the small with a click of the mouse and link people in the address book to assignments and appointments. Routine reference information or essential notes

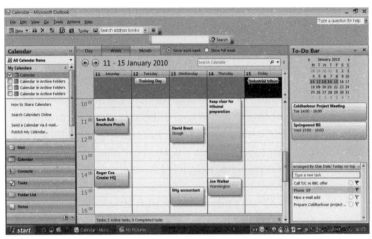

Figure 2.3   Microsoft Outlook Calendar

are easily incorporated, and it is simple to track time and cost. Depending on your software and networking setup, you may also be able to assign tasks to others and be kept updated on progress, or to compare diaries online when seeking suitable times for a meeting. You do, of course, need a computer to hand in order to access all these facilities, although this is much less of a drawback than it used to be given the ever greater power and smaller size of laptop and netbook computers, and the increased sophistication of other portable devices such as personal digital assistants and smartphones.

Smartphones and personal digital assistants (PDAs)

Personal digital assistants were devised as a means of carrying all necessary information for personal organisation in an easily pocketable electronic device. They all incorporate standard PIM features – address book, calendar/appointments schedule, task lists and jotter. Nowadays they are typically bundled with a mobile phone to produce the so-called smartphone, and offer the facility to receive and send e-mails on the move, access the internet, make voice recordings and carry out some simple office tasks. Most mobile phone producers now have their upper range smartphone models, and all allow for relatively easy synchronisation with data on your PC by wireless communication or cable link. For inputting information, they use either a touch sensitive screen with handwriting recognition, a miniature keyboard or a virtual on-screen keyboard. None of these is particularly conducive to the input of large amounts of data but, for those who want to use their smart-phone/PDA as an alternative to a laptop, there are folding keyboards that can allow for a near normal typing experience. However, a netbook might well serve as a more satisfactory alternative for such users. A netbook is a very small portable PC, typically weighing about 1 kg, which has minimal specifications by today's standards, but is quite adequate for all routine office applications, e-mail activity, internet access and PIM software.

What system is the best?

It all depends on how you like to work. Paper-based systems are clearly much less powerful in terms of cross referencing, and require a degree of duplication. They lack the facility for automatic reminders and it's easy for items to get lost. On the other hand, inputting or extracting information from computer-based systems can interrupt the flow of other activities, and there may be new skills to learn, such as the distinctive letter formation required for handwriting recognition. And don't underestimate the gizmo factor. If you're into gadgets, it is possible to get carried away by what your hardware or software is capable of doing, rather than what you actually need it to do.

There is no doubt that we are increasingly turning to technology to assist our personal organisation, but it is not yet time to declare an end to paper-based methods. Even the most technologically committed of us will admit to tasks where we prefer to use paper – for example, when mapping out the activities to be included within a project before getting down to detailed planning. For my part, whilst I use the PIM software on my netbook extensively, and synchronise the information it contains with my desktop PC and phone, I will always keep a notebook to hand, often preferring to make a scribbled note to be entered later rather than interrupt the flow of other activity in order to interact with an electronic device.

'To do' lists

Whether a 'to do' list is scribbled on the back of an envelope or flashes up on your computer screen, its essential purpose is the same, and so are its potential drawbacks. It can be a simple yet powerful tool or a meaningless exercise. The difference lies in how you apply it, and there are some important points to bear in mind if 'to do' lists are to work for you.

The first question is: where does your list come from? It's not going to be a huge amount of help if it consists of just a collection of items that pop into your head each morning. Such a list is likely to focus too heavily on attractive or urgent but not necessarily important issues. Your planning will benefit if you have some form of master list from which your daily and weekly lists are drawn. This is relatively straightforward if you have given appropriate attention to the long-term dimension of your activities – breaking down projects and major objectives into the tasks required to ensure their completion.

Separate your master list into different categories to keep it manageable and in order to be able to construct, edit and view a particular area of activity in isolation. If you are using Outlook, go to 'Edit/Categories' to change the master category list. Get rid of some of the irrelevant pre-formatted ones, and set up new ones as the need arises.

Difficulty with 'to do' lists most often occurs as a result of unrealistic expectations of the number of tasks that can be completed within a given time period. Compiling a list of tasks provides a sense of getting to grips with one's workload and it's easy to become carried away. The consequence is a list that can be daunting and may feed a tendency towards procrastination. Stress about tasks not achieved replaces the positive buzz that compiling the list provided, and items on the list become almost permanent features – rumbling on from day to day and week to week until finally the whole exercise is abandoned.

So, it's very important that you build a habit of achieving the things you have listed. Keep your expectations reasonable and don't allow items to roll on day after day. Setting due dates for key tasks will help you structure your progress towards the completion of projects and major objectives, but allocating dates to every task at the time you first enter them in your planner or PIM can lead to logjams, with too many tasks from different areas of activity popping up at once. Your master list will be more manageable if you get into the habit of reviewing it regularly and setting due dates for less time-critical tasks in the week or fortnight before you expect to achieve them.

Activity

Before leaving this section, take a few moments to reflect on how you currently plan and track your time. What changes might you usefully make to the tools you are using at present?

Scheduling your time – estimating time requirements

You start the day with, let's say, a dozen items on your 'to do' list. What confidence do you have that at the end of the day they will all have been crossed off? Not a great deal unless you have made some estimate of how long each task is likely to take, and fitted them in with the other commitments that make up your day. It isn't just about the confidence and credibility boost that comes from achieving what you set out to do, although that should not be underestimated. Estimating time requirements of tasks allows you to use the available slots in your day appropriately. If you have half an hour between commitments, you want, wherever possible, to fill it with a half-hour task. Discovering that a task you thought was going to take half an hour is really going to take an hour may result in additional time spent refocusing your attention when you eventually come back to it.

You will never achieve time estimation perfection. Tasks will contain unforeseen elements, and we all have a tendency to overestimate the time taken to complete those tasks we dislike, and to underestimate the ones we like. But taking a moment to think about what is involved with a task before you pop it into your schedule can greatly help the management of your working day.

Slotting tasks into the day

Your day is likely to be made up of fixed commitments – appointments and regular scheduled elements – and flexible ones – the tasks on your 'to do' list. Having roughly estimated the time you expect these tasks to take, you can then get an idea of when you will hope to fit them in. Don't seek to rigidly plan your whole day in advance, and don't spend a lot of time on the process. It should be a quick and simple way of giving your day shape and balance, fitting tasks into appropriate time slots, not a bureaucratic exercise. Half-hour time slots are a manageable way of dividing up your day, although for some smaller tasks you may want to think in terms of quarter-hour slots. Group several minor tasks – five or six phone calls for example – into a half-hour slot. Allow a bit of padding in your time estimates for some of the inevitable calls and interruptions. There is a great satisfaction boost to be had from completing a task in less than the time you expected it to take, but you also need to maintain your cool when tasks are taking longer than planned. Above all, stay flexible and deal with whatever the day throws at you.

Activity – improving your scheduling accuracy

If it isn't your current practice to estimate the time that tasks will occupy, start by setting a rough estimate alongside each item in your 'to do' list. Once you are under way, monitor the accuracy of your time planning for several days:

- Give a rough time estimate to every task on your 'to do' list.
- When you complete the task, enter the actual time taken alongside the estimate.
- Compare the differences over the period of a week.
- Are there any patterns of consistent over- or underestimation?
- Are there reasons you can discern for the inaccuracy?
- What can you do to improve accuracy?

Procrastination

Some element of postponement is both inevitable and necessary in a busy life, but we give ourselves needless stress and may greatly reduce our effectiveness if we indulge in habitual procrastination. It's probably the biggest time management problem for a great many of us, and we need to take a look at why it occurs and what we can do about it.

The first difficulty is that we don't admit to ourselves what we are doing. We present ourselves with excuses such as:

- 'I haven't got all the information I need to tackle this job.'

- 'I don't have time at the moment to do it justice.'
- 'There are other deadlines that are more pressing.'
- 'If I do nothing with this, it will probably go away.'

We tackle the easier items and those that may be superficially more attractive, while some of the most important tasks remain undone. But the stress of not tackling a particular task is often greater than that involved in carrying it out. We waste time and energy worrying about the things we have not done when with a little more resolve they could be consigned to the out-tray.

But it isn't just a matter of telling ourselves to show greater determination. Procrastination may have become a deeply ingrained work habit that we have nurtured and indulged over the years.

The reasons why we postpone tackling tasks may be complex and varied. They include:

- boredom;
- lack of confidence in our ability to complete the task;
- fear of making a mistake;
- perception of the task as difficult or unpleasant in some way;
- lack of clarity about the requirements of the task or the resources needed to complete it successfully;
- anxiety about the possible consequences of actions required within a task.

And putting tasks off to another day is not the only problem. Just as prevalent is the tendency to delay getting down to the main job in hand by using minor tasks as self-generated diversions. We know what we should be spending our time on, and we may even be relishing getting our teeth into it, and yet we experience a curious resistance. We seize upon any excuse to direct our attention elsewhere. Checking e-mail inboxes, grabbing a cup of coffee, texting a friend or dropping in on a favourite internet site can suddenly become much more pressing than the task we should be involved with. We tell ourselves, 'It will only take a couple of minutes to do this', but once the interruption has been made, it leads on to other equally pressing little chores, and half an hour is frittered away in the blink of an eye. In our modern environment, characterised as it is by immediacy of electronic communication, routes to distraction are much more prevalent than they used to be, and the incidence of procrastination appears to be rising as a consequence. In a recent study carried out by the University of Calgary, it has been noted that the average self assessment score for tendency towards procrastination has risen by 39% in the last 25 years. The author of the study Professor Piers Steel says, 'It's never been harder to be self disciplined in all of history than it is now.'

Unfortunately, procrastination is a habit that tends to get worse the more we indulge it. Tasks routinely postponed may become impossible to fulfil.

Strategies for beating procrastination

As with most problems, recognition of its existence is the first step to overcoming it. Keep an eye on any tendency to feed yourself the sort of excuses listed at the start of this section. Observe yourself over the coming days and look for any signs of resistance to particular tasks. Ask yourself what the reasons are – fear and anxiety, boredom, uncertainty, perfectionism – the same ones will not always apply. Once you have identified the reason(s) it's easier to select the most appropriate strategies for overcoming the problem:

- **Get the pain balance right.**
  The prospect of carrying out the tasks you are avoiding involves an element of perceived pain, but not doing them involves actual pain. The problem is that while the perceived pain is envisaged as a big hit – one that gets worse the longer a task is postponed – the actual pain of not carrying out the task comes in the form of a steady low-level irritation. You need to adjust the balance between the two, so that the pain of not doing

the task outweighs the perceived pain of doing it. You can achieve this by:

- clarifying in your own mind the consequences of procrastination in terms of loss of control over your life;
- introducing penalties for non-performance;
- making a public commitment or opening yourself to be held to account for non-completion of certain tasks.

Tackle perceived pain by noting the frequency with which tasks you have been avoiding turn out to be less fearsome than expected, and use this knowledge as a reference to help overcome future anxieties.

• **Similarly, address the pleasure side of the equation.**
What pleasure do you get from procrastination? The answer, generally, is none. How will you feel if you fulfil the tasks you are currently resisting? Imagine the end of a week in which you have achieved everything you set out to do, and visualise what completion will feel like.

• **Ensure that anything making it on to your 'to do' list is a firm commitment and not just a vague intention.**
Keep the list short to start with, and review what you have achieved at the end of every day and every week.

• **Don't allow postponed tasks to build up a head of steam to the point where they become even more difficult to tackle.**
Arrange your 'to do' list so that the tasks you dread most are the ones you deal with first. Your reward will be a day or a week that gets easier as it goes along.

• **Schedule specific times in your diary for tackling tasks you don't like or are resisting.**
Ritualise tedious recurring tasks by including them at set times in your schedule until they become embedded routines that demand little mental energy.

• **Tackle boredom by allowing yourself short controlled breaks at predetermined times or when a certain proportion of a task has been completed.**

But maintain your discipline to ensure the breaks don't become a distraction from the main task.

- **Recognise when the resources at your disposal are sufficient to achieve a good job.**
Don't strive after perfection.
- **Give yourself immediate positive reinforcement for successfully dealing with tasks you have been resisting.**
This may consist of a mental pat on the back, a positive diary entry or some meaningful pleasurable reward.
- **Look for an easy point of entry to those tasks where you have been unsure how to get started.**
The important thing is to make a start at whatever point.
- **Short bursts of concentrated activity – just 5 or 10 minutes at a time – can work well as a way of overcoming inertia.**
They serve to overcome the psychological obstacle posed by a difficult or daunting task. You can amaze yourself by how much it is possible to achieve in just a few minutes, if you punch holes in a task by this means. Suddenly it is no longer daunting and you are starting to achieve the momentum needed to carry you towards completion.
- **Divide large and complicated tasks into bite-sized chunks so that they appear less formidable.**
- **Set your own deadlines for tasks where they are not externally imposed.**

Activity – ask yourself

- **What are the tasks over which I regularly procrastinate?**
- **What are the reasons for this?**
- **What strategies can I usefully adopt to overcome it?**

Meeting deadlines

There are five main reasons why deadlines aren't met:

- **The deadline is unrealistic to start with.**
- **The deadline is inadequately planned for.**
- **The person responsible for meeting the deadline is unable to get started on the task.**
- **The person responsible for meeting the deadline is let down by others.**
- **The person responsible for meeting the deadline spends more time on the assignment than necessary.**

Dealing with unrealistic deadlines

The best time to counteract an unrealistic deadline is when it is being set. If you think that you are being asked to work to a deadline that isn't feasible, show that you have thought through the timescale rather than simply rejecting the proposal out of hand. Adopt a positive problem-solving attitude. Set out the stages that will need to be met in order to deliver on time, and explore whether there are any ways through the difficulty – such as additional resources which would help you to meet the required timescale – or whether it is possible for the deadline to be reconsidered. Unfortunately, deadlines are seldom set in a perfect working world, and while the timescale for a project may seem reasonable when viewed in isolation, the chances are that it will cut across other assignments that also have deadlines. One tactic you can adopt with the person setting the deadline is to ask them whether it takes priority over the other deadlines you are working to, and if so, which they would wish you to set back in order to meet the timescale on the new job. Remember too that some of the least realistic deadlines are the ones we set ourselves. Just as we pile too many activities into our daily 'to do' lists, so we overestimate just what we will be able to achieve in the coming weeks and months.

In some circumstances there may be deadlines that are unrealistic but not subject to influence. They may arise from the requirements of external bodies, regulators or clients. If affected, the only solution is to address the other demands on your time to free the space that will allow the deadline to be met. Once again, it is essential that you do this early enough to make a difference.

Before you start work, make sure you are completely clear what is required of you, what resources you have at your disposal, and what additional support you may call upon if necessary. Failure to deal with these issues is a frequent cause of missed deadlines.

Planning to meet your deadline

OK, so you have accepted the deadline. You now need to plan your implementation of it. Break the assignment or project down into a series of stages which will lead you to a successful conclusion and try to estimate the amount of time each will take. Calculate the number of working days between now and the planned completion date and ask yourself what you will need to do each week (or each day if you are dealing with a short deadline) in order to achieve it. Build in sufficient slack to allow for unexpected events and delays, and make sure that, in estimating the time needed for each stage, you have taken account of the other commitments which have a call on your time.

As you work towards completion of your project, use the finishing point for each of the stages as a milestone – a point at which you can monitor your progress, and ensure that you are on track. Use them also to give yourself the positive reinforcement necessary to maintain motivation. If you are able to get ahead of your schedule at any time, resist the temptation to slacken off. Use the time to build in some additional flexibility at the end of the project. The tidying up elements are often the ones most likely to be underestimated.

Inability to get down to the work

This tendency frequently accompanies poor planning. It may be that you are not sure you have all the information you need in order to make a start or just that the finish date seems such a long way off. You convince yourself that you have ample time and will be sure to get down to it in a day or two. People will often procrastinate over the start of a project because they lack confidence in their ability to succeed at it, or they are unsure where to start. If affected by this, then cast aside worries about tackling the task at the beginning, and simply pitch in at whatever point appears to be the most straightforward. The momentum you gain from making inroads into the task will usually outweigh any inefficiencies resulting from stages tackled out of order.

Avoid being let down by others

Often, completion of a project or assignment will not be entirely in your hands, and you will be reliant on input from others if you are to meet your deadline. Once again good planning is the key to ensuring that others don't present problems for you. Recognise that they will have priorities of their own, which are likely to differ from yours. Let them know in plenty of time what it is you require from them and the date by which you will need their input. It generally helps to set this date a few days before you actually need it so that any laxity on their part doesn't throw out the schedule for any subsequent work you need to do with their input. Make your requirements as clear as possible so as to avoid any misinterpretation.

Don't go over the top in seeking perfection

This is another failing which signals lack of confidence. It may be a matter of research or information gathering which is out of proportion with the task in hand and results in the person undertaking the task becoming bogged down and unable to see the wood for the trees. Or it may be unwillingness to let go of the project – relentlessly honing and polishing it with the aim of producing the perfect job. You need to avoid both these tendencies and recognise the point at which further effort does not produce a commensurate return.

Activity – ask yourself
- What difficult deadlines have I been faced with recently?
- What were the reasons for the difficulty?
- How do I need to change my way of working in order to address such problems in future?

Time management and projects

I have referred to projects several times in this chapter, and it is worthwhile spending a few minutes considering the particular demands that projects place on your time. In the context of this chapter, we shall regard the term 'project' as including any undertaking leading to a significant outcome, where successful achievement requires completion of a number of elements over a period of time. It may be an assignment you carry out entirely by yourself, or may involve the input of others.

One of the major difficulties with project activity from a time management perspective is that it has to take place alongside other work. Harking back to the breakdown of work by importance and urgency which we used earlier in this chapter, it is usually Sector B activity – important but not urgent – and for that reason may be pushed off schedule by other, more urgent pressures which are actually less important. Care in planning and tracking your projects is therefore vital.

Whole books are written on project planning and management, and there are some complex techniques necessary for handling projects with hundreds of time-critical tasks, possibly involving the input of numerous individuals or organisations. This book, concerned as it is with personal organisation, clearly cannot enter that level of complexity, but there are some basic principles that apply to all projects. Any project should embody five stages:

- **initiating – clarifying general aims, setting out objectives;**
- **planning – breaking the project down into tasks and activities; deciding in what order they should be accomplished; determining the timescale, deciding what resources are needed;**
- **executing – carrying out the work, co-ordinating the input of others, resolving difficulties;**
- **monitoring – ensuring the schedule is progressing according to plan; redefining, rescheduling and reallocating resources as necessary;**
- **completing – finalising the results, reviewing the outcomes.**

The organisational skills required for successfully completing projects are largely those covered in other parts of this book – setting objectives, delegation, meeting deadlines, estimating time requirements – but you should give particular attention to defining tasks and the order in which they are to be carried out. This is something that requires you to ask a number of questions:

- **What activities are needed to achieve this objective?**
- **In what order should they be carried out?**
- **Do any of them need to be broken down into smaller tasks?**
- **What resources are required to accomplish them?**

The most common problem in defining tasks is a tendency to accept the first answers that come up. Don't expect, even with straightforward projects, to pull out all the answers at once. Revisit your first attempt. You are quite likely to see new elements that were not immediately apparent.

Depending on the complexity of the project, it may be necessary to identify sub-projects, each containing its own set of tasks and sub-tasks. Some tasks will be dependent on the completion of others, or may have others dependent on them. Delays in completing such tasks can throw out the whole project schedule, so it is important to clarify start and finish dates for them, and identify what room there is for slippage.

If you are planning a project which has a lot of interrelated tasks, project planning software can greatly facilitate the process. It will allow you to alter timings and relationships and to add or move tasks until you are satisfied with the project schedule. You can then make use of powerful charting and tracking facilities offered by the software. However, these packages are not simple and may involve a significant learning task if you are unused to project planning conventions. For this reason a PIM is to be favoured over free-standing specialist software for those projects that are not too complicated.

Summary

If you are to organise your time more effectively, you need to:

- **be aware of the way your time is currently spent;**
- **be able to plan your activity over different time frames;**
- **select planning and tracking tools that work for you;**
- **estimate the time required to complete tasks;**
- **eliminate procrastination;**
- **adopt an organised approach to meeting deadlines;**
- **plan and track project activity.**

3

Understand the way you work

After planning and prioritising your work and taking steps to manage your time, the next point to consider is the way in which you set about it. In this chapter, we shall examine four features of your approach to tasks which can greatly improve effectiveness: scheduling tasks at appropriate times; working in short bursts to maintain concentration; mobilising the power of habit; and dealing with decisions systematically.

Schedule tasks at appropriate times

It is likely that your workload consists of a variety of different tasks. You will have limited jurisdiction over when to carry out those that are dependent on the availability of others, but for the majority of tasks there will be some flexibility on timing. Most tasks will fall into one of three broad groups:

- *maintenance tasks* – those routine jobs which are essential to keep you functioning properly, staying informed, dealing with the normal inflow and outflow of information, organising your workspace, completing routine correspondence;
- *people tasks* – negotiating, participating in meetings, persuading, reviewing performance, networking, resolving complaints, presenting, training, interviewing;
- *creative, planning and problem-solving tasks* – preparing plans and project briefs, writing reports, analysing information and drawing conclusions, finding solutions to problems, generating new ideas.

These are just a few examples. Depending on the nature of your job, there will be others appropriate to you.

Recognise the demands that different tasks place on you

Generally speaking, the maintenance tasks will make the most limited energy demands. Later in this chapter we will look at how many of them can be made even less demanding by harnessing the power of habit. Creative planning and problem-solving tasks will normally require the greatest amount of concentrated attention and also larger blocks of time because of the need to get yourself up to speed before you are able to make significant progress. People tasks may be of long or short duration, but are frequently the ones which make the greatest demands on emotional energy. Those that may involve an element of confrontation are particularly draining. If you have several of these tasks, try tackling them together – one after the other. The head of steam you build up to tackle the first helps to carry you through the subsequent ones and, overall, you will find it less emotionally draining than having to gear yourself up for each one individually.

We are all familiar with the idea of a body clock which
regulates our sleeping and waking. Anybody who has ever
worked a night shift or crossed time zones will testify to the
havoc caused by its disruption. But we give much less attention
to the peaks and troughs of alertness that occur throughout our
waking life, and which vary significantly between individuals.
Needless to say, the alertness cycles in your day can have a potent
effect on performance and it pays to schedule your most
demanding tasks at the times you are best able to deal with them.

What are your best times?

We are accustomed to describing ourselves in general terms –
'I'm a morning person', 'I do my best work in the evening' – but
have you ever looked at your work patterns in more than the
most cursory terms? You may have become locked into a way of
working not particularly suited to your body rhythms as a result
of difficulties in organising your day. You may assume, for
example, that evenings are the times when you do your best
planning and problem-solving activity, when in fact those tasks
have been squeezed into that end of the day because you have
found it impossible to give them the concentrated thought they
require amid the distractions and interruptions of normal
working hours. If, as a result of better organisation, you are able
to deal more effectively with interruptions, you may find that you
can readdress your assumptions about the best times to take on
particular tasks.

Start by examining the way you currently work with some
simple analysis. Record your daily activity each day for a week.
This can take the form of your daily 'to do' list, supplemented by
those other routine activities that make up your day. Mark each
item with three symbols:

   1. a letter to indicate the type of task: 'm' for maintenance, 'p'
      for people, 'c' for creative;

2. a number between 1 and 5 to show the time of day you carried it out: 1 = early morning, 2 = late morning, 3 = early afternoon, 4 = late afternoon, 5 = evening;
3. plus or minus signs to indicate perceived energy levels: ++ = high energy, + = moderate energy, – = fairly low energy, – – = very low energy.

At the end of the week, examine the outcomes to see whether there is any pattern of activity that warrants change. Are there intensive tasks you are currently attempting at perceived low spots in your day? Are there easy maintenance tasks that would more usefully occupy those low spots? Make adjustments to your schedule in the following week and note any improvements in performance.

Why you can't always rely on the same body rhythms

Your normal pattern of energy peaks is a good guide to the times when you should schedule your most demanding tasks, but don't regard it as infallible. On the days when you are slightly under the weather, or at the end of an exhausting week, there may be no appreciable energy peaks and any sort of demanding activity is a struggle. If you have any choice in the matter, don't labour on with a difficult task that is not working for you. In these circumstances you are unlikely to break through into sunny pastures. Far better to switch to a more routine maintenance task and return to the intensive one when you are rested and re-energised. Beware, however, of using this as simply an excuse for procrastination.

On the reverse side of the coin, when things are going particularly well don't stop just because you have reached today's target. If you have energy and creativity to spare, and a task is flowing for you – go with it. Keep your schedules flexible and be prepared to listen to your body.

Fit the task to your available time

There are some tasks that you can only set about if you have a significant chunk of time – you need to gather resources around you, get yourself into the right frame of mind and make sure that you are free of interruptions. Other tasks you can dip in and out of more quickly. Don't waste your time trying to gear up for a long-slot task when you only have a short slot available. Keep some quick pay-off tasks handy for those spare moments when somebody due for an appointment is running late, when a meeting doesn't start on time, or while you are waiting for a train.

Maintain concentration and motivation

Our capacity for sustained concentration will vary according to the nature of the task, the time of day and the degree of distraction, but even at the best of times it is finite. When tackling lengthy, mentally intensive tasks we need regular breaks that allow us to maintain our focus. But as we have already noted, it's easy to slip into disorganised habits, whereby breaks become diversions that take on a momentum of their own and prevent us getting back to the main task in hand. Successfully negotiate your way through lengthy tasks by adopting the following rules:

1. Make breaks short and reasonably frequent, but never take them on impulse.
2. Set yourself a succession of clear, timed targets, each with an element of challenge that is demanding but achievable, to see you through the overall task. A period of between 30 and 60 minutes for each target is generally the most workable. You may be able to concentrate on some tasks for a longer period, but for most attention will be on the wane after this time. A tough challenge to be achieved in

an hour is less daunting than one that you expect to take two, and you're also less likely to cut yourself any slack. It's possible to blast away at a task for this length of time and achieve more than you thought possible.

3. The timed element to your target is important for a disciplined approach to the job, but go for the achievement of your target task rather than sticking rigidly to the time allocation. If you achieve it in less than the target time, so much the better – give yourself a pat on the back. If it takes a little bit longer than you thought, then stick with it to see it through. Only if you find that a task is taking a lot longer than you anticipated or you hit a complete brick wall should you reassess your expectations. In such a situation you might set a lesser target to be achieved within the chosen time period, or look for a way of getting past the obstacle that has blocked your progress, perhaps seeking a different angle on the problem or moving to a new part of the overall task with a view to returning to the problematic area later. Do not permit an unexpected hitch to be an excuse for downing tools.

4. At the end of each target period, before you take a break, set your next target task and make a start on it for just a few minutes. That way, you will be returning to work in progress, and the effort of refocusing will be significantly less.

5. OK, you can take that break now. Just a few minutes doing something different is generally enough. It might be a quick and easy maintenance task, an undemanding phone call or an opportunity to stretch your legs or relax your eyes after a sustained spell of computer activity. What matters is that it should be different from the other task you have been doing, and you should not allow it to develop into a lengthy diversion. If other supplementary tasks arise, give them their own slot on your 'to do' list and get back to the main job in hand.

Mobilise the power of habit

You only have a finite amount of energy each day and you want to be able to expend it as productively as possible. But the chances are that all sorts of trivial and time-wasting tasks are using up your available resources and preventing you pushing forward those larger projects which require sustained concentration and effort. By enlisting the power of habit, you can free up the energy you need to devote to the intensive tasks which will really make a difference to your effectiveness. If you pride yourself in bringing an element of creativity to your work and have an instinctive antipathy towards anything that smacks of becoming a creature of habit, console yourself in the knowledge that having some habits and routines in your day can give you more energy to tackle the creative things at other times.

Consider the routines you go through when you get up in the morning – cleaning your teeth for example. They have become ingrained – part of the way you start your day. Your thoughts are elsewhere while you are doing them – listening to the radio or planning your day – and you don't worry about them. They demand no mental energy. There are tasks in your working day which can be turned into the equivalent of cleaning your teeth. They may not permit quite the same level of mental detachment, but they're tasks which currently use up unnecessary energy. They vie with all the other demands upon you for a place on your busy schedule – you have to decide when to do them, and worry about them when they are not done.

A number of the general organisational tasks featured in this book may usefully be made the subject of habits and routines. They include:

- **updating your schedules for the following day/week – Chapter 2;**
- **handling incoming information – Chapter 4;**
- **keeping your workspace clear and organised – Chapter 6;**

- carrying out routine filing and computer housekeeping
  – Chapter 7.

There will be others specific to your job. On the flip side of positive habits which can free up our energies for more important activity are current negative work habits which condemn us to ineffectiveness.

Frances Craig is a classic example of a messy desk worker. Although disciplined and organised in many other ways, she works amid overwhelming and distracting clutter. She is aware of the amount of time she wastes looking for things among the piles of paper which totally obscure her work surface, and she is conscious that with a little more discipline she could clear her desk on a daily basis and work more effectively. She engages in periodic purges during which important material is liable to get ditched with the junk, but so far she has not succeeded in building up a regular desk clearing habit.

What fixes habits?

Habits, positive or negative, are fixed by repetition and reinforcement. Everybody is aware of the role that repetition plays in habit formation, but often we fail to persist for long enough to make a new routine automatic. We need to remember also that repetition will only work if it is accompanied by reinforcement.

Reinforcement can be positive or negative. Often overlooked examples of positive reinforcement include a word of congratulation (even if it comes from yourself) or simply the boost that comes from crossing an item off your 'to do' list.

Negative reinforcement may come in the form of unwelcome discomfort. Some reinforcers are stronger than others. Those that are clear and immediate tend to have more effect than those that are vague and in the future. In the case of Frances and her desk habits, the consequences of any different way of behaving are vague and indefinite by comparison with the immediate reinforcement provided by her current work habit, which she perceives as the ability to move quickly and easily from one job to another with the minimum of preparation or clear-up time. To change her behaviour she needs to make a deliberate connection between different habits and their consequences, and to work on reinforcing it every time she exhibits the desired behaviour.

Habits are also bolstered by your environment – including your own attitudes and perceptions of self, those close to you and the prevailing culture in your place of work. Frances's view of herself as a busy, creative type is a part of the background to her behaviour, as is the tendency in her workplace to view an empty desk as an indicator of somebody with not enough to do.

It follows from all this that simply deciding you are going to introduce new routines into your working day is no guarantee of success. You need to address the environment in which your current behaviour flourishes, and work on nurturing and reinforcing the desired habit until it becomes automatic. It won't happen immediately but the end result will be worth a bit of persistence.

Activity – ask yourself

- Which of my current work habits contribute to effective performance?
- What are the work habits that limit effective performance?
- What new habits could I develop to improve performance

Tips for changing habits

- **Start thinking in positive terms about the habit you are working to develop.**

  Associate it with desirable outcomes – the chance to free up time and energy for creative and enjoyable jobs – rather than focusing on the boring and mundane nature of the task itself.

- **Similarly, associate new habits with positive aspects of your self-image.**

  They are essential parts of your creativity and decisiveness rather than routines that bring out your bureaucratic traits.

- **Change the environment in which those habits you wish to change currently flourish.**

  For example, coincide a change in desk organisation with an overall purge on your workspace.

- **Remember that immediate positive reinforcement is what fixes new habits.**

  This might come in the form of crossing an item off your 'to do' list, rewarding yourself with a desirable outcome (now I can go home, now I can go to lunch) or simply congratulating yourself on a task completed. Give yourself immediate positive reinforcement every time you engage in the new behaviour.

- **Hang your new routines onto key times in your working day.**

  First thing, just before lunch, immediately after lunch, just before you go home. Associating them with constant landmarks makes them less likely to be overlooked.

- **Continue reinforcing and monitoring the new behaviour until it is established.**

  Include the new work habit on your daily 'to do' list for several weeks and reward yourself for sticking to it.

- **Find ways of providing timely reminders for those newly introduced routines that will not occur on a daily basis.**

  If you use an electronic means of managing your commitments, you might employ the recurring appointment facility to prompt you at the appropriate times.

- Make use of checklists, forms and templates to reduce the mental effort involved in completing routine tasks.
- Don't try to take on too much at once.

Be satisfied with incremental steps, nurturing new habits until you are convinced they are established before turning your attention elsewhere.

Sharpen up your decision making

Decisions come before action. If you suffer from indecisiveness or poor decision making, it will inevitably have an effect on the quality of your personal organisation. And if you are fussing over decisions that don't need to be taken or that could be delegated to somebody else, then you will inevitably have less time and energy for the things that matter.

There are a number of things that may get in the way of effective decision making:

- fears and anxieties;
- availability of information and other resources;
- conflicting timescales;
- the behaviour of others.

Fear

Fear, as we have already seen, is a factor in procrastination. Decisions are often postponed or referred elsewhere out of fear of making a mistake. Anxiety about the process of implementing a decision may be just as important as choosing the right course of action. You may know what is the right thing to do, but the prospect of carrying it out is frightening. Possibly it holds the prospect of unpleasant encounters with others. Difficult decisions to do with people – disciplinary matters, for example – are often bucked for this reason.

Information

Information is the cause of so-called 'analysis paralysis'. Either there is insufficient information to make an informed decision – often an excuse used to justify procrastination – or there is so much that the person responsible for the decision is overwhelmed. There is a fear element to information gathering too. On the one hand lies the fear that acquiring further information may throw up additional complications. On the other is the equally damaging fear that if you stop information gathering you may miss an essential nugget that would set you on the right track. You need to keep data acquisition in proportion to the importance of the issue to be decided, and learn to recognise the point at which you have obtained sufficient data to define and weigh the options adequately, without tipping over into additional work, producing rapidly declining benefits.

Timing

You don't need to be told about windows of opportunity. Making the right decision at the wrong time can be as damaging as making the wrong decision at the right time. Some decisions have to be taken quickly, and dithering will allow the moment to pass. But take care not to rush decisions which need careful consideration – perhaps because there are several steps to them, or because they have implications for other activities. There may also be short- and long-term dimensions to the issue you are considering. Biting the bullet in favour of a long-term solution is generally to be favoured over repeated sticking-plaster responses.

The behaviour of others

Decisions are not taken in a vacuum. For the most part they will impact on others who will come with their full quota of prejudices, hobby horses and baggage in the form of perceptions of status, role and reputation. They may need to be convinced of the benefits and perhaps to take ownership of the decision. Ignore all this and you might as well forget about making the decision at all.

A systematic approach to decision making

There are five parts to making any serious decision:

1. Clarify what you are about
This is best accomplished by asking yourself some questions:

- **Why do I need to make this decision?**
- **What are the goals I wish to achieve?**
- **What information do I need to make this decision?**
- **What will happen if I don't do anything?**
- **Who do I need to involve?**
- **What is the timescale?**
- **What resources are available to me?**

2. Identify the available options
This is a point at which short circuits often occur. In the process of identifying options, a superficially attractive one pops up and the focus moves away from exploration of all possibilities and towards justifying why this particular solution should be chosen. Even with decisions that require a speedy response it is worth taking a little time to ensure you have identified all the possible options before you start to evaluate them.

3. Weigh the pros and cons of each option
A simple approach is to adopt a balance sheet strategy for this task. Draw a line down the middle of a sheet of paper and, for

each option, list the pros on one side and the cons on the other. Keep the goals of the exercise very clearly in front of you as you do this. Don't treat the pros and cons as if they all carry equal weight. You may want to give each a weighting on, say, a one to ten scale. But remember that you cannot expect to come to a conclusion simply by allocating and adding up weightings. Some points may have absolute rather than relative significance. A single point against may be of such weight that it eliminates all the points in favour. Beware also of what may seem to be overwhelming pros. The novelty value of some options may lead to the cons not being adequately explored.

4. Pare the options down to the point that you are able to make a choice.

Some options will have been immediately dismissed by failing to meet the goals or having overwhelming points against them. For those that remain, you need to take account of risk surrounding their implementation. How likely is it that factors beyond your control may affect the successful implementation of the decision? And what is the balance of risk against potential gain? Also consider elements such as how the decision will be sold to those who have to implement it.

5. Sell the outcome

Actually taking the decision may not be the point at which the job finishes, rather the point at which it starts. It is often then a matter of communicating the decision and gaining the commitment of others, and this is where a lot of good decisions come unstuck. Communicating the decision is a selling job and the principles of effective persuasion apply:

- **Approach the task from your audience's point of view. Address their aspirations and fears.**
- **Establish credibility by demonstrating a clear plan for the implementation of the decision.**

- Sell the benefits of the decision rather than dwelling too much on the reasons for it.
- Anticipate any objections that may be raised and prepare convincing responses to them.

Now move on

Recognise that you can never get it right all the time, particularly when there are people involved. At the time you make the decision, its implementation lies in the future. Circumstances may change for reasons you couldn't have predicted at the time you made the decision, and because of that you do need to keep the consequences of decisions under review. But having chosen the best option, you need to implement it and move on, without constantly revisiting the options to worry whether you have made the right choice.

Summary

Effective organisation of your workload will be improved if you are able to:

- recognise those tasks which place the greatest demands on you and schedule them when you are at your most energetic;
- fit the task to the time you have available;
- build up positive work habits and eliminate negative ones;
- take a systematic approach to decisions.

4

Organise information

- Does the amount of incoming information you are required to deal with seem to be constantly growing?
- Do you find yourself going over the same material more than once without seeming to take it in?
- Would you like to be able to read faster at the same time as improving your comprehension?
- Do you have difficulty keeping up to date with the reading you feel is necessary for effective performance of your job?
- Do colleagues bombard you with forwarded e-mails, reports and copies of other written material that you don't need?
- Do you find yourself unable to decide what to do with documents and messages you receive?
- Do you put items to one side to be dealt with later?
- Do you retain magazines, reports and web references intending to read them, but never get around to it?
- Are you plagued by junk mail?

- **Do you find difficulty locating a piece of information which you know is somewhere within a particular book or report?**

If you haven't answered yes to any of these, then you are a pretty unusual being in today's workplace. Recent surveys have shown that throughout the developed world, people are struggling to cope with the vast quantities of information they are required to handle in their jobs and that widespread stress and productivity decline are a result.

In this chapter we will look at a systematic approach towards handling incoming information. We will examine ways to reduce the volume of what comes your way, and techniques to help you read, sort and assimilate it more efficiently.

Identify the important information

Some information is immediately recognisable as junk. Other items scream their importance. But it isn't always simple to separate with certainty the vital from the marginal. Use the following questions to help determine the value of whatever information comes your way:

- **Does this information relate to a key element of my job?**
- **Would I choose to receive or keep this information if I had to pay for it?**
- **What is the worst that would happen if I ignored it?**
- **Is it information that I need at this point in time. If not, can I access it easily should I want it in future?**
- **Eighty per cent of the value comes from 20 per cent of the information. Is this item in the top 20 per cent?**

You cannot be sure of getting it right every time, but resist the temptation to deal with this uncertainty by a strategy of 'if in doubt, treat it as important'. Information perfection – always having exactly the right information available at the right time – is not possible. While the availability of good information is important to the effective discharge of your job, more information will not guarantee better performance. Beyond a certain point, additional information will have a declining marginal value, and information has no value at all if there is so much of it that it cannot be properly interpreted and understood. So, recognise that you have no hope of taking in everything, focus on the important, and accept that your judgement will be imperfect. Remember also the need to discriminate between the urgent and the important. Items requiring a speedy response may assume a greater importance than they deserve. An unimportant matter which has been left unattended for several days does not become any more important because its deadline is approaching. It simply becomes more urgent.

Adopt a systematic approach

There is a common myth, perpetuated by some time management programmes, that every item of information should be handled only once. It doesn't work like that in the real world. For a variety of reasons, you might need to come back to a document. An item may genuinely need to be mulled over or put together with other information before you can make a sensible decision upon it. It may be more efficient to deal with some items in context with others on the same subject. What about the document which makes you angry? Although a response fired off immediately may do something for your blood pressure, you are likely to produce a more effective reply, and one less likely to escalate confrontation if you wait until you have cooled off. Some items may need repeated handling in the process of drafting a complex document. If it is possible to touch a document only once, then this is clearly what you should aim for, but don't become too hung up on the 'one touch' approach. Ensure that no document or message goes back onto the pile, and that every item receives a positive action on the first touch. This action should be one of the following five Ds, summarised in Figure 4.1.

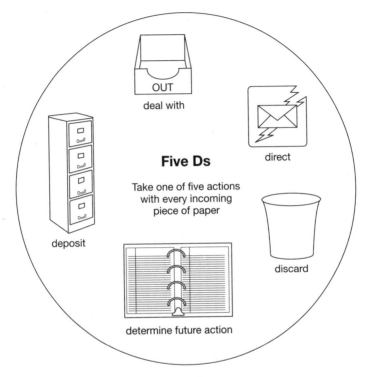

Figure 4.1 The five Ds

Discard

The quickest way to become bogged down with information is by wasting time and energy reading material of little or no benefit to you. So, the first question to ask yourself is 'Do I want this at all?' It should be quickly apparent if an item has no use for you, but we are often reluctant to consider the bin until we have waded through a document. There is also a tendency to put to one side documents that one is unsure about. There they form a mounting pile with other items, gathering dust or clogging up your inbox – occasionally being revisited in half-hearted attempts to clear the backlog. Remember that most information has a limited shelf life. A useful rule of thumb is – if it doesn't seem valuable today it isn't likely to tomorrow.

Deal with

Provided that you are able to do so quickly and effectively, you should deal with items when they first come to you. An immediate action on a document is satisfying and stress-relieving. It also means that you will not have to spend time refreshing your memory before you can act upon it in the future. Where it is not possible to deal with an item immediately, then at least determine what action you will take and when.

Determine future action

When dealing with paper, never return an item to the pile. Make sure you have a system for bringing forward items on which you will need to act, and make a point of noting the action required, or the possible options, on the document or a sticky note attachment. A concertina file marked with the dates of the month makes a useful 'bring forward' device. Place the item in the compartment corresponding to the date when you wish to revisit it. Use project files for items which need to be worked upon with others as part of a larger task.

You can adopt a similar approach with e-mails. Use the 'flag for follow-up' facility in Outlook, which allows you to select the sort of action required and choose a date on which you will receive a reminder. You may also want to add a comment to the e-mail in order to assist you in dealing with it when the time comes. Don't simply return it to your inbox after you have done this. Place it in an appropriate folder or, if your e-mail software doesn't have a follow-up reminder, set up a folder for actions pending and make a point of visiting it regularly.

You will need to exert some discipline in respect of items determined for future action:

- **Do not use it to avoid one of the other four Ds.**
- **Do not move items on beyond the day you have originally set for action.**
- **If you have a 'to read' file, don't let it become a general dumping ground.**

Direct

Don't send items to others just to get them off your own desk or out of your inbox, or because you don't know what to do with them. You will only add to other people's information burden, further belabour the internal communication system and possibly fill the bins of others more quickly than your own. Think about why you are redirecting the item and what you want the other person to do with it. A brief note will help them to assimilate and act upon it more quickly.

Deposit

Storing an item in whatever form of filing system is not an action to take because you don't know what else to do with it. Be sparing in what you file. We will look at ground rules for filing in Chapter 7.

Avoid overload

However effective you become at handling the stuff, you will not achieve all that is possible unless you also take steps to reduce the volume of information that daily arrives for your attention. Even if you only glance at the majority of it, you may be wasting considerable time and effort.

The most important step you can take is to examine your own behaviour. Your maxim must be 'do unto others as you would have them do unto you'. The more you distribute information unnecessarily, the more you are likely to receive it in return.

Here are some other ideas:

- Don't invite junk mail by handing out your details unnecessarily. And don't waste time on the junk mail you receive. You can dump the majority without even opening it.
- Remove your name from mailing lists if they provide you with nothing of value.
- Consider internal communications. Circulation lists within organisations are often unnecessarily large. If you can do so without creating political difficulties for yourself, ask to be left off circulation lists for documents which do not concern you in any way.
- Examine subscriptions to periodicals, ezines and other online journals. Those which have not yielded anything worthwhile in the last six months may be due for cancellation.

Over-copying

Over-copying is a form of workplace insurance. When you're not sure what to do with a document or who may need sight of an e-mail, the easiest solution is to engage in multiple copying – sending it to everybody who might conceivably have use for the information therein. You have achieved two things – the offending item is off your hands, and you have also absolved yourself from any responsibility for failure to communicate. However, you have added to the information burden of others and have not necessarily communicated anything. If you aim to protect yourself by over-copying to colleagues, they are likely to respond in the same way.

Read more efficiently

The speed and efficiency with which you can assimilate incoming information is a significant factor in your ability to organize your workload. It has been estimated that people in information-intensive jobs may spend up to a third of their working day in activities involving reading, and yet most of us are not as efficient readers as we might be. The average reading speed is between 200 and 250 words a minute. With some simple techniques and practice this can easily be raised to 500+ without detriment to your understanding. Slow reading speeds are not particularly a function of education or intelligence. Many able and well-educated people read at or below the average speed. Even if you already read quickly, there is generally scope for improvement. It is a myth that only by reading slowly can we expect to understand material. Better comprehension can go hand in hand with faster reading.

What is my current reading speed?

If you want to estimate your reading speed, simply choose an appropriate passage, at least a page in length, that you haven't previously read. Try to read it at a normal pace consistent with understanding the content, but take an accurate note of the time it takes you. Next, estimate the length of the passage by multiplying the average number of words per line by the number of lines it contains. Use the following calculation to estimate your reading speed in words per minute.

$$\frac{\text{number of words in the passage} \times 60}{\text{time taken in seconds}} = \begin{array}{l}\text{reading speed}\\ \text{in words per}\\ \text{minute}\end{array}$$

Why do we read slowly?

When we read, our eyes do not move continuously across the page, but rather hop several words at a time through the material. It is during the stationary period (fixation) at the end of each hop that the reading occurs; and it is, of course, the brain which does the reading rather than the eyes. In simple terms, we might think of the eyes as a still camera taking a series of shots which the brain then interprets. The main reasons for slow reading speed are:

- **limited number of words encompassed in each fixation;**
- **fixations of longer duration than necessary;**
- **involuntary or deliberate back skipping over material already read.**

A fourth factor in slow reading is a tendency to mentally hear the words as we read. This is known as sub-vocalisation and is believed to originate from the approach used when we first learn to read – actually speaking the words aloud. The problem with sub-vocalisation is that it restricts us to little more than the speed of the spoken voice, which is typically around 150 words a minute. Sub-vocalisation can be greatly diminished if never entirely eliminated.

Training yourself to read faster is a matter of technique and practice. There are numerous books and courses available on the subject, and in the space available here, it is only possible to introduce a few techniques. With a little determination these should bring about a significant improvement.

Using a pacer

Most speed-reading programmes advocate training with some form of pacing technique which forces your eyes to move on and eliminates lengthy pauses or back skipping. You can use your index finger or the blunt end of a pencil, moving it swiftly across the page just below the line of text you are reading. At the end of the line, move the pacer quickly to the start of the next line, and so on. Maintain a pace above that which feels comfortable and refuse to allow your eyes to go back over what you have already read. At first you may feel that you have taken in little or nothing of what your eyes have passed over, but with practice you will find increased levels of comprehension as well as speed. It has been shown that faster readers actually understand more because they are able to tune in to the general thrust of the piece they are reading, whereas slower readers become bogged down in detail.

It is natural to feel some anxiety about the process of taking in larger blocks of material at each hit, but in many aspects of our daily lives we absorb significant blocks of information at a glance. We register road signs, hoardings and headlines without stopping to 'read' them and we can significantly increase the span of words which we take in on each fixation. It is commonly thought that fast readers read down the middle of the page and that their span therefore encompasses the whole line of text. This is, however, very difficult to achieve except with text in columns. Fast readers may take in six or more words per fixation, and their eyes will remain in the central third of the page rather than following a line down the centre of it.

As your reading speed increases, you should find yourself able to progress to a smooth zigzag movement of the pacer, taking in more than one line at each pass, and without the necessity to lift the pacer from the page (Figure 4.2). Avoid reaching the point where you are forcing yourself along and are more conscious of the process of reading quickly than of what you are taking in. Once you have reached a reasonable speed you may wish to relinquish your pacer.

Figure 4.2   As speed increases, adopt a smooth zigzag motion with the pacer

Other techniques

Increasing your reading speed will, of course, take a little time and you may wish to tap into the structured practice of a speed reading course. Whether or not you choose to do so, here are some further techniques you can employ almost immediately to improve both speed and understanding.

Preview for increased understanding

We read much more quickly and effectively if we are slotting information into a known framework. A few moments spent establishing that framework can pay significant dividends. The approach which follows assumes you are setting out to read a substantial document such as a book, periodical or report. It can be adapted for shorter documents:

1. Before starting on the main text, skim through the Contents page, Introduction and Summary (if there is one) or Conclusions.

2. Next, flick through the document, establishing an appreciation of the main structure and argument. Look particularly for section or chapter summaries. They are excellent for getting quickly to the guts of a document. Failing that, read the first and last paragraph of each section or chapter. These will often introduce and summarise the arguments contained therein.

3. Now, when you move to read the document properly, you will be filling in the gaps rather than starting with a blank sheet. You will know which are the parts you need to concentrate on, and which you can blast through or skip altogether.

Vary your pace

It goes without saying that texts vary in their levels of difficulty, but many people maintain the same pace regardless of what they are reading. Even within a document there will be some sections which are more difficult to absorb than others. Don't be afraid to slow down where the text requires it, and to power through the easier passages.

Focus on what is important

At some point in most documents there will be digressions from the main argument, things which you already know, things you don't need to know and straightforward padding. The best way to approach any reading task is with the question 'What do I need from this?' foremost in your mind. You will read more quickly and remember more, if you can focus on the elements which are necessary for you in whatever task you have to fulfil. Don't approach the printed word with too much reverence. The writer does not necessarily know any more than you do on the subject.

Develop scanning techniques

When you need to find a particular piece of information, you can move to it quickly by scanning. Focus your attention solely on the information you wish to locate and let your eyes follow your finger as you run it rapidly down the centre of each page from top to bottom. This process should be considerably faster than your paced reading, and if you are focused on the information you want to locate, it should leap out at you when you get to the relevant part of the document. You will improve with practice. Of course, scanning is no substitute for using an index where one exists.

Be selective about what you read

Never try to read everything that lands on your desk or in your inbox. That way lies madness. You need to be ruthlessly selective and stick to those things which add value to your role. And remember – people who put reading matter aside for an indeterminate time in the future when they will be less busy are destined to be forever disappointed.

Catching up with reading

Catching up with reading is not a task that imposes itself on your schedule and consequently the pile just grows. Use the suggestions from the previous chapter to find a low-energy time in your week when you can build in a regular reading catch-up session. Provided you keep it fairly short and don't have unrealistic expectations of what can be achieved in each session, it can serve as a useful and rewarding variation on your other activities, and one that will not overly disrupt your flow or general productivity. It's important for motivation that when you turn to your reading file, you are not confronted with a teetering stack of dust-covered volumes or a daunting array of online documents. So have a ruthless clear-out before you put your new system into action. Ditch the less-relevant material and any periodicals more than six months old, so that you can start with a task that is manageable. Keep an easily transportable reading file to hand for those occasions when you are travelling by public transport or waiting for the commencement of a meeting that has been delayed.

Use your memory

The value of what you read declines pretty rapidly if you can't remember it. Fear of forgetting results in a number of negative habits. We hang on to documents of minor significance, read slowly and back skip over the printed page. For effective information handling we need to trust our memories. The more we use them, the more reliable they will be. If you do nothing to assist your memory you will forget up to 80 per cent of what you read within 24 hours of reading it. Here are a number of simple techniques which can help you remember better:

- **The level of recall you require will vary.**
  For some information, it will be sufficient for you to remember simply that it exists and where to find it. With other information you will need a grasp of the general subject and main ideas. At the highest level you may need to recall information in detail or even verbatim. Assist your memory by selective reading and awareness of the level of recall you need.
- **Read with a question in your mind.**
  What do I want to achieve from this? How does it fit into what I know already? All learning and remembering is a process of association.
- **Try to see the overall pattern to what you are reading.**
  We remember much better if we can see the general structure and the broad ideas into which the detail fits.

- **Use the information in some way.**

Summarise it in your own words, make margin notes as you read, communicate the information to others, or act on it.

- **Recognition, the process of remembering with assistance from an external stimulus, is much easier than pure recall.**

Make conscious associations which will help you to pull detail from your memory. It has been shown that the more bizarre the association, the more likely it is to work. Silly mnemonics, ridiculous visual associations, they all work.

- **Review important information to fix it in your long-term memory.**

You will gain the most advantage by quickly reviewing material shortly after acquiring it (10 to 15 minutes) and again a day later. Experts recommend further review after a week and a month for reliable long-term recall.

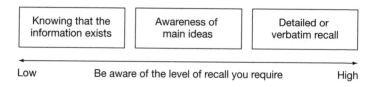

Figure 4.3   Level of recall

Summary

Dealing effectively with information is a matter of:

- separating the important information from the junk;
- maintaining a systematic approach with all incoming information;
- handling all incoming information as sparingly as possible;

- taking steps to reduce unnecessary incoming mail;
- building up your reading speed and comprehension;
- using memory techniques and review to assist your recall.

5

Organise the way you work with others

Much of our working day is spent in some form of interaction with others. The way you approach these interactions can have a considerable impact on your effectiveness. In this chapter we shall look at meetings, delegation, overcoming distractions and interruptions, helping others to be more organised, and learning to say no.

A strategy for meetings

The time-wasting potential of meetings is immense. In many organisations you can spend hours every week in meetings that achieve very little. But for all that we moan about them, we keep on holding the things and attending them. Why?

People go to meetings for reasons other than to make decisions. Meetings cultivate a sense of one's importance – closeness to the wheels of power. They are an opportunity to make an impression on your colleagues. Not being invited may smack of exclusion. I have known people, left out of meetings that had almost negligible relevance to them, become incandescent over what they perceived as deliberate downgrading attempts. There is also a social element to meetings, and they can be less demanding than some other forms of work activity. Once you are in the meeting you're cocooned, safe from phone calls, interruptions and the tough problems that inhabit your inbox. OK, so meetings are boring, but you can play a few mind games with colleagues or just let your attention wander.

Why do we hold meetings? Meetings are held to:

- **impart information;**
- **elicit views;**
- **stimulate new ideas;**
- **motivate a team;**
- **reach decisions.**

There are more effective ways of passing on information than dragging people together into a room and subjecting them to one of those verbal memo meetings where only the senior person speaks and everybody else sits mute. There are also non-meeting ways of consulting and eliciting views. The creative or brainstorming meeting has long been seen as a way of exploring new solutions to problems, but studies have shown that frequently people are more creative when working individually. Similarly, one-to-one reinforcement and coaching can often achieve more than a motivational team meeting, and the non-challenging culture ('groupthink') developed by some meetings may not favour good decisions.

So, in the face of all this, whenever the prospect of a meeting comes up, the first question to ask yourself is: Do we need a meeting at all? Unfortunately that question isn't asked often enough. In many organisations, meetings go ahead at regular intervals regardless of whether they are really needed. Business expands to fill the agenda and you have all the ingredients of a classic talking shop.

Assuming that you decide a meeting really is necessary, what can you do to ensure that it achieves its purpose without devouring too much of the participants' time? Unproductive meetings generally fall down on aspects of planning and management.

Inadequate planning

There may be no agenda, a poorly prepared one, or no clear purpose to the meeting. Information needed to make sensible decisions may not have been produced, or participants may have failed to read papers provided in advance.

Poor management

There may be inadequate control of timing, failure to keep discussion on the agenda, inability to control people intent on riding their pet hobby horses, inability to draw conclusions out of the discussion.

Here are some pointers aimed at overcoming these and other meeting problems.

Ten points to remember when calling a meeting

1. Frame the agenda as clearly as possible. Identify the specific questions the meeting needs to address rather than setting open-ended topics.
2. Indicate a target time allowance for each agenda item and stick to it as closely as you can.
3. Limit attendance to those who have something to contribute on the matters under discussion and the authority to implement decisions. Generally speaking, the more people there are at a meeting, the longer it will take.
4. Schedule meetings immediately before lunch or at the end of the day. People's anxiety to get away will override their verbosity.

5. Try not to schedule meetings in your own work area. You will find it harder to get away from any post-meeting hangers-on.

6. Start the meeting at the scheduled time. Waiting for late-comers encourages them to repeat the misdemeanour, and irritates those who have arrived on time.

7. Don't allow discussion to be sidetracked onto matters not on the agenda. If they are important they can be dealt with at a subsequent meeting.

8. Don't waste time discussing matters where there is inadequate information to make a decision. Agree responsibility for obtaining and reporting the necessary information and postpone the discussion to a future date.

9. Avoid the practice of Any Other Business at the end of meetings if at all possible. It is often used by people too lazy to prepare an item properly for the agenda, and can result in bad decisions made on the basis of inadequate consideration. It can also kick into touch all your efforts at timing discussion.

10. Ensure that as soon as possible after the meeting, a record of the outcomes is prepared. The quicker it is done, the easier the task. Detailed minutes are generally unnecessary, and only give people something to argue over at the start of the next meeting. Action notes are more useful. They should include: a) what the meeting agreed; b) who has responsibility for actioning those agreements; and c) dates by which they should be actioned.

Ten points to remember when attending a meeting

1. Make sure beforehand that you know what the meeting is aiming to achieve. If the aim doesn't seem clear, question

the convenor about it. This should have the effect of clarifying objectives, leading to a more productive meeting, or demonstrating that a meeting isn't actually needed.

2. Ask to be excused any meeting which does not appear to have any relevance to you. You have to be wise to the politics of this. If your boss is the one calling the meeting, diplomacy may require that you go. Often, however, the convenor simply hasn't given sufficient thought to meeting membership. Questions like 'What are you hoping I will be able to contribute?' can lead them to think again.

3. If only one item in a meeting is relevant to you, ask whether it can be placed near the beginning of the agenda so that you can be spared the rest of the meeting. Be aware, though, that this tactic sometimes sparks a bidding war on the part of others similarly affected.

4. Always read the agenda and any papers before a meeting and, without taking up an inflexible position, clarify your thoughts as to what you would like to achieve from the meeting.

5. If you expect your arguments to meet with some opposition, a little subtle lobbying in advance may be useful. Other participants may not have given the meeting much advance thought, and people are more inclined to stick with a view that they take into the room than they are to be won over by something they hear during the meeting. Handle lobbying carefully though. If the other person sees your approach as an attempt to exert undue influence, you risk actually turning them away from your point of view.

6. Think in advance about what you will settle for if you don't get what you want. Most people will not have thought about a fallback position. Skilfully presented – that is before it is apparent to everyone that you have lost the argument – it can be a disarming way of getting at least a substantial part of what you want.

7. Don't overcommit yourself. Meetings are a bit like auctions. In the to and fro of discussion it's easy to get carried away and make undertakings you later regret. There's a natural wish to make a good impression in front of colleagues, but don't let yourself be tempted into taking on too many responsibilities or offering unrealistic target dates for completion of work.

8. If you find yourself locked into excessively long meetings, arrange for an 'important' appointment, or vital interruption, which will require you to leave before the end. Don't do it too often, or you will arouse suspicions.

9. You can help a weak chairperson by summarising the arguments of others and pulling the threads of a discussion together to facilitate decisions. By all means draw people's attention to overruns on time, but take care to ensure that you are not a guilty party. We tend to overestimate the time that other people have been talking and underestimate our own loquacity.

10. Try to set some regular times when you are available for meetings attendance and make them known. If you are able to make this work, it can help prevent meetings breaking up your working week in such a way that you are unable to get to those tasks which require concentrated activity over a number of hours.

Alternatives to meetings

As noted at the beginning of this section, there are more efficient ways of doing some of the business traditionally reserved for meetings, and these are assisted by modern technology. Some of the possibilities are as follows:

Using e-mail effectively
Dissemination of information to groups is quick and easy with e-mail. Outlook includes tools like voting buttons, to assist

consultation or the collection of views. Alternatively you may
wish to draw e-mail communication together into a forum such
as those available through the 'Groups' facility offered by the likes
of Google and Yahoo. These enable participants to post issues for
discussion, respond to the comments of others and upload files
to share.

Instant messaging

In many circumstances this can be a hugely irritating
interruption to other work, but as an alternative to meetings it
has considerable advantages, offering as it does a simple and
immediate means of sharing ideas and answering questions.

Collaborative services and applications

For activity that doesn't require real-time interaction, these
may provide a valuable workspace in which notes can be
exchanged, tasks assigned, documents shared and worked on
collaboratively. There are a number of services available – the
subscription-based PB Works is an example – and a reasonable
degree of collaborative activity is also possible through free
services such as Microsoft Office Live. Additionally, some
software packages such as project management applications will
also allow for members of a team to collaborate at a distance
almost as effectively as if they were meeting together.

Videoconferencing

This is now within the scope of even the smallest business,
given the plummeting cost of required hardware and the
availability of fast internet connections. Where individuals
would otherwise travel some distance to attend a meeting, the
savings in time and travel expenses will rapidly outweigh any
setup costs.

Delegate

Edward Newton reckons to work an average 58-hour week. The company he works for has been going through major changes recently and Edward's job has been closely associated with those changes. He is aware that he tries to do too many things himself and that some tasks could be passed on to other members of his team, but he feels that those he can trust are themselves overloaded. It's also his belief that, in the short term, the time taken to brief and coach somebody else would exceed the time he is currently spending on these tasks. His problem is exacerbated because, in a situation of change, he is unsure how long his workload will remain at the present level, and hence he is reluctant to pass on responsibilities only to take them back later. At the back of his mind there is even a slight worry that he may need his heavy workload to justify his existence in any future restructuring. From time to time he gets so overloaded that he simply has to dump jobs on colleagues with wholly insufficient briefing or assistance.

There are lots of Edwards in every area of work – people whose competence is being stretched to the limit by competition, change and restructuring. They are suffering from the catch-22 situation where they know they ought to delegate more but feel they haven't the time to do it properly. But for anybody who wants to get organised and stay on top of the job, delegation has to be part of the recipe.

The first important point about delegation is that it should not be a knee-jerk reaction to your own overload. It isn't just a matter of offloading tasks you don't want to do, but a contribution to overall productivity by placing responsibility and the necessary authority and resources where they can be discharged most effectively. You will have difficulty with delegation if you're not prepared to invest the time in setting arrangements up, if you can't trust your colleagues or if you cannot believe that anyone else is able to do the job as well as you.

At one time delegation was always seen in terms of tasks being passed to more junior colleagues, but in these days of flatter organisational structures, there is an increased tendency to think of sideways delegation – the movement of work between colleagues at the same or a similar level. This is really more about trading responsibilities than delegating them in the traditional sense. We all have differing skills and work preferences. If a colleague is able to fulfil an area of your responsibility more effectively than you, and you in turn can bring your skills to an aspect of his or her job, then it makes sense to co-operate. However, the fact that the arrangement is between colleagues at the same level should not be a reason for any less care in the setting-up process.

Five steps to effective delegation

1. Decide what you will delegate

The choice of responsibilities to delegate will normally centre on those things that others may do more quickly, more cheaply or more expertly than you, or tasks that can readily be performed within the context of another person's existing job. There will generally be core elements to your own job that you should not consider delegating.

2. Choose the right person

Beware of the natural tendency to load the willing horses or to delegate tasks only to those who have fulfilled similar work in the past. The reasons for delegation are not only about easing your own workload but about giving new development experiences to others.

3. Prepare the ground

You have to be ready to prepare colleagues for what you want them to do. Time to do this is often an issue, but it is a matter of short-term pain for long-term gain. If you don't set the arrangement up properly, you are likely to have disgruntled colleagues feeling they have been dumped on or people unclear about what is expected of them. You will need to set clear objectives using the SMART formula we discussed in Chapter 1. Let your colleague know the parameters of his or her authority and what support you will be able to provide.

4. Sell the benefits

It's important to look at these from the other person's point of view. There may be training and development benefits to him or her in taking on a new responsibility, enhancement of career prospects, variety and challenge, or opportunity to use particular skills. Be prepared to spend time talking to the person concerned, seeking responses to what you are proposing, and responding constructively. If your colleague can feel that the setting-up process is a collaborative one, he or she will be more committed to taking it on.

5. Stand back

Let the other person get on with it. One of the most common delegation problems is a tendency to interfere or reject the work because it is not being done in exactly the way you would have done it. You need to work hard to avoid this, particularly if you have been doing the job yourself for some time. You should make it clear that you are available to offer support, but that day-to-day responsibility is down to the person to whom you have delegated it. If you don't, it will remain essentially your responsibility, for which you have simply contracted out part of the donkey work. When problems occur, they will wind up back on your plate, and your colleague will not achieve the development benefits that delegation can offer. Of course, the authority you delegate is not limitless, and the person taking on the responsibility should be aware of its limits, but he or she also needs the freedom to operate and sometimes to make mistakes and learn from them.

Overcoming distractions and interruptions

Interruptions and distractions impose heavily on our ability to organise work schedules. Not only is there the actual time lost through the interruption but, more importantly, the effort of getting back to the original task and re-focusing attention. The extent to which we are distracted from our work has become much more acute in recent years as a result of technological advances. We live and work in a world where we are constantly connected, often simultaneously, to multiple communication vehicles – e-mail, the web, mobile phone calls, texts and instant messaging – not to mention our face-to-face interactions with people and the impact of old-fashioned landline telecommunication. In many settings, this ever-present connectedness is regarded as an essential aspect of working life, and multitasking has become the order of the day. But multitasking is not something that human beings are terribly good at. We manage it well enough if we're concerned with activities that demand only minimal attention, but we find it very much more difficult when engaged in those requiring creativity, abstract thought or sustained focus.

A study in 2007 conducted by Microsoft Research and the University of Illinois found that it can take up to 15 minutes to productively resume a challenging task when interrupted by something as simple as an e-mail. And interruptions can result in reduced accuracy of memory too. They interfere with the business of processing information between short-term and long-term memory. It has been found that in some occupations workers are having to switch their attention every few minutes, and the detrimental effects of this are becoming so widely acknowledged that a new term – 'continuous partial attention syndrome' – is increasingly used to describe them.

Of course, not all distractions and interruptions are technological in nature. Some are social, often by people who are themselves engaged in procrastination over tasks they want to escape. You may even be the source of the distraction. It is very easy to convince yourself that you just have to make a phone call, get a coffee or check your favourite blog, and you will be back on track in a few minutes. Once the pattern of work is disrupted, you find other pressing chores and the minutes stretch to an hour or more, after which time it is much harder to pick up the threads.

You will never be able to get rid of interruptions entirely, but you can do a lot to reduce them, and to make those remaining as brief and purposeful as possible. Aim to cut out all bar the most urgent and important – those things that impinge on the key purpose of your job or the organisation you work for, and where the consequences of failure to give the matter your immediate attention may be of detriment to either.

The great benefit of e-mail, voicemail and text messaging should be their time independence, and you will certainly be far more productive if you are able to deal with them at times of your choosing rather than when they arrive. Research has shown that people handle messages and other interruptions much more effectively if they occur at natural break points in the other activities they are carrying out. If it is possible for you to do so, set two or three times each day when you will routinely check and deal with calls and messages, and be disciplined about sticking to this routine.

Unfortunately for many readers, this may seem like an unachievable luxury. If you work in a culture where there is an expectation of immediate responses to calls and messages, it may feel almost impossible to free yourself of constant interruptions. But if you want to get the important things done, it is essential that you look for ways to balance accessibility and productivity. You might consider an approach that mirrors the triage techniques used in emergency medicine – filtering out those messages which have to be dealt with immediately from the rest that can wait until a more convenient time. One way to get a handle on the important issues quickly is to set your e-mail software just to download headers rather than the full message. You reduce the temptation to deal with each message immediately if another action is required before you can read it, and you can usually tell which messages are important from the header information. It's also a good idea to turn off audible notification of incoming messages and texts. There's nothing more likely to make us interrupt what we are doing than the urgent beep of an arriving message.

Changing email settings in Outlook
To download headers only.
1   Go to Send/Receive Settings
2   Define Send/Receive Groups
3   Edit

To turn off audible notification.
1   Go to Tools Menu
2   Options
3   Email Options
4   Advanced Email Options
5   Uncheck 'Play a sound' box

To set up rules or alerts.
1   Go to Tools menu
2   Rules and Alerts
3   New Rule
4   Check messages when they arrive
5   Next
6   Check box alongside chosen condition, and click underlined value to edit rule description
7   Next
8   Select actions to apply and edit rule description of action if necessary
9   Finish
10 Apply

You may also like to think about giving yourself e-mail free periods during the day – times when you can work uninterrupted on tasks that require your complete attention. If you're concerned about ensuring accessibility for important messages even during your e-mail free periods, you might consider setting your e-mail software to give you an audible or on-screen alert only when messages from particular senders or those containing certain words in the header are received. You might, for example, let people know that to reach you straight away, they should include the word 'immediate' in the subject line of their message. If you have an auto-responder facility, you might consider setting up a message along the following lines: 'Thanks for your message. I'm busy on a task that requires all my attention, and can't respond immediately. I check my e-mails regularly and will get back to you today. However, if it is vital that you have a response straight away, please re-send your message with the word *immediate* in the subject line and I will deal with it immediately.' An alternative strategy to the use of 'rules and alerts' (which won't work if the software is set to download just headers) is to designate a second e-mail address for urgent messages and to set this up for immediate notification.

Fifteen more ways to reduce interruptions

1. Be clear about what you are trying to achieve in your day. Following the advice on planning and tracking your time in Chapter 2 will help you to rate the importance of distractions and interruptions, and keep your focus on what matters in terms of overall productivity.
2. Consolidate tasks such as sending messages and making phone calls to avoid each one becoming a separate interruption to your workflow. You will handle them more effectively and save significant amounts of time that may currently be spent re-focusing after each interruption.
3. Return phone calls at times when people are unlikely to be keen to enter lengthy conversations – just before lunch, or at the end of the day when they want to get

home. Alternatively, set timed calls when agreeing to phone back – 'I've got five minutes to spare between appointments at four o'clock. Can I phone you then?'

4. Give thorough briefings when passing on tasks to others, so that they have less need to come back to you with follow-up questions.

5. Clarify instructions and address any weaknesses in procedures that lead to repeated queries, and deal with requests quickly to avoid people chasing you.

6. Set regular times each day when you will deal with those tasks that require uninterrupted concentration and will be unavailable for meetings, calls and other interruptions. Stick to it rigidly and, with luck, others will come to respect your interruption-free zone.

7. If you work in an open plan environment and have no other way of signalling times when you don't wish to be interrupted, consider using an 'OK to Disturb/Please Do Not Disturb' card by your desk.

8. Help to foster a climate conducive to effective work by treating colleagues as you would have them treat you. Avoid excessive copying or forwarding of unimportant e-mails to others, and don't expect people to refrain from interrupting you, if you're in the habit of interrupting them.

9. Take breaks at predetermined times. Build them into a constructive work routine, so that they start to work against self-inflicted interruptions.

10. Remember that cluttered workspace is a potent source of visual distraction. Follow the advice in the next chapter to help reduce any tendency to flit from task to task.

11. Consider working from home when you have a task that needs concentrated thought. Provided that your home doesn't have its own distractions, you may be able to achieve more in a few hours of peace than is possible in a busy workplace.

12. Explore a reciprocal arrangement with colleagues whereby you divert your phone to others so that they can take messages when you need to work on a task interrupted, and you do the same for them at other times.

13. When carrying out work on the internet, beware of following hyperlinks that lead you to other interesting but irrelevant material.

14. If you have senior colleagues who consider that every summons constitutes a reason for you to drop everything, be prepared to work patiently and diplomatically with them to improve awareness of the effects of their behaviour. Share with them, at times other than when they are interrupting you, the measures you are taking to manage your day, and demonstrate the effectiveness of your strategy by your results.

15. Free yourself from the belief that you have to be constantly connected if you want to work effectively. While there are many benefits to today's instant communication culture, there are equally considerable disadvantages. As noted earlier, effective multitasking is largely a myth. Only by switching off or otherwise limiting sources of interruption for at least part of your working day, will you be able to present yourself with the space to carry out tasks requiring concentrated attention.

Keeping interruptions brief and productive

When interruptions are unavoidable, aim to make them as short as possible. Here are some ideas:

1. Put a time limit on the interruption. Let the person interrupting you know that you can only spare, say, five minutes. Some experts suggest keeping an egg timer on your desk and using it to remind your visitor to get to the point quickly.

2. Risk being considered rude by not inviting interrupters to sit down.
3. Position office furniture and desk to avoid giving your working area a 'please walk in and sit down' appearance. This is particularly important if you are in an open-plan office.
4. Encourage colleagues to come with a bullet point note of what they want to talk to you about. This helps you to tune into the issue quickly, helps them to focus their thinking, and deters more frivolous interruptions because of the preparation involved.
5. If you have difficulty drawing interruptions to a conclusion and sending visitors on their way, think about your body language and the verbal cues within a conversation that allow you to wrap the meeting up without unduly offending the other person.

Help others to be more organised

In spite of all your attempts to organise your own schedule and way of working, the disorganisation of others can still throw you into confusion, so it's worth giving some attention to strategies for greater organisation among those around you.

Disorganised colleagues

Lecturing people on their lack of organisation will seldom lead to much more than grudging compliance and, as none of us are wholly without fault, it will often be accompanied by privately exchanged grumbles of, 'He/she's a fine one to talk'. Getting people to articulate their own difficulties and the tactics they can adopt to resolve them is likely to be far more productive. This is generally a matter of asking the right questions in a setting which encourages reflection – a one-to-one meeting or appraisal, for example. Help your colleagues to focus on one thing at a time, and give immediate positive reinforcement in the form of praise and encouragement when you see them working to change their ways. Reinforcement is a very powerful motivator for change, so don't wait until the altered behaviour hits you between the eyes. Actively look for things to praise. Peer pressure can also be a strong influence on individual behaviour. It may be worth considering whether there is mileage in a whole-team initiative aimed at working towards improved effectiveness.

Disorganised boss

A disorganised boss can be a nightmare to work for, but don't treat his or her weaknesses simply as gripes to be shared with other colleagues over coffee. Provided you go about it the right way, you can make a difference, but you will need to be content to work on those aspects of your boss's behaviour that you can influence, and put up with those you can't. Make sure that your own work and organisation cannot be faulted, and avoid full-frontal challenges unless you have another job to go to. Here are five traits frequently displayed by disorganised bosses with suggestions on what to do about them.

Inability to make a decision

Remember that bosses are seldom masters of their own destiny. Rather than fuming over what might seem at first sight to be indecisiveness and negativity, make an attempt to understand the politics in which they are operating, and give them the ammunition to fight battles further up the line. Recognise also that your boss may have difficulty tuning in to an issue which has been the focus of your attention for days or even weeks. Be prepared to talk through the thought processes which have led to the conclusions you have reached.

A tendency towards snap decisions

This species lies at the other end of the scale from the

indecisive boss and will deal with any question by delivering top-of-the-head certainties. Anything that smacks of thinking time or consideration of alternatives is for wimps. Never approach such a boss with an open-ended question unless you want to find yourself saddled with unworkable solutions and impossible deadlines. Work out the options beforehand and present them with a cogently argued thumbnail guide. The boss will normally want to be credited with a decision, so build in at least one point where there is a choice to be made between alternatives, neither of which would be disastrous.

Inability to end meetings

If your boss is the sort of person who finds it difficult to conclude a meeting, make sure that you have another pressing engagement which allows you an escape route within a reasonable time.

Failure to set clear objectives or focus on the important issues

Clarify your aims and objectives by writing down what you think they are and getting your boss to confirm them. In one-to-one meetings with your boss, provide a written summary of the issues for discussion and list possible solutions to problems.

Inability to remember what he or she has asked you to do

Develop a practice of taking notes whenever you meet to discuss tasks, and sending your boss an action note detailing what you have agreed to do, as soon as possible afterwards.

Learn to say 'no'

A large part of organising yourself is about remaining in control of your workload. If you always say 'yes' to requests that come your way, then you lose that control. You over-burden yourself, with the resultant stress, and by saying 'yes' to unimportant requests you may find yourself unable to fulfil key objectives. There are a number of reasons why saying 'no' may be difficult:

- **You don't want to appear unwilling and spoil your prospects.**
- **You're concerned that you might displease others or hurt their feelings.**
- **You underestimate the increased pressure you will be under as a result of saying 'yes'.**
- **You simply don't realise that saying 'no' is an option.**

Of course, you don't want to get a reputation for negativity – a knee-jerk 'no' may be worse than a knee-jerk 'yes'. If you are in the process of establishing yourself in a new job or interest group, you may need to say 'yes' more often than is good for you. But it is important to be able to draw the line skilfully and assertively, and recognise that it is impossible to please everyone all the time. Decide which requests you need to turn down by asking yourself:

- **How does this fit with my main objectives?**
- **Will my prospects be affected if I don't do it?**
- **What else might I need to drop or postpone in order to undertake this? What will be the effect of that on other objectives?**
- **Will doing it result in any detrimental lifestyle effect – significantly increased stress, unreasonable intrusion on my leisure time?**
- **Will I miss out on any opportunity to develop a new skill if I don't do this?**

Try a balance sheet approach – pluses on one side, minuses on the other – where the choice is difficult.

How to do it

There are three ways of approaching 'no'.

Aggressive approach
Complains loudly about being overburdened and taken for granted. Accuses the person making the request of being unreasonable, rants or bursts into tears.

Timid approach
Responds to the request with mumbled attempts to delay a decision. Leaves the person making the request unclear about whether 'yes' or 'no' has been said. Wastes energy fretting about the request and ends up doing it resentfully.

Assertive approach
Indicates pleasure at being asked, but explains succinctly and politely why he or she is unable to respond positively. Suggests possible alternative ways of getting the task done, and specifies what support he or she can offer to whoever takes on the task.

Needless to say, the third is the approach you should aim for. The person making the request is under no misapprehension about your response or the reasons for it, but does not come away from the encounter angry and brow-beaten; and you do not damage your reputation for helpfulness and positive thinking.

Take particular care with requests where the commitment asked of you is not immediate, but comes at some time in the future – a request to make a presentation at a conference, for example. When the event is three months away, it's easy to be over-optimistic about the time you will have to fit in the necessary preparation. But as the day approaches and you find your schedule ever more crowded, the additional task assumes the status of an unwelcome addition to a heavy workload, and you end up resentfully turning out a rush job which doesn't do you justice. Awareness of priorities, clarity about your schedule and control over planning are the ways to ensure that you don't fall into this trap.

Summary

You can achieve greater effectiveness in those aspects of your work that involve others by:

- **helping to ensure that the meetings you attend are as productive as possible;**
- **delegating in the right way and for the right reasons;**
- **actively working to beat distractions and interruptions;**
- **recognising that you can help others to be more organised;**
- **learning to say no assertively.**

6

Organise your space

The way you organise your space can have a considerable effect on your productivity – saving time, preventing fatigue, allowing you to complete tasks more quickly. But it's very easy to become accustomed to a working environment that is less than ideal, so take a few minutes to look at your office with a fresh eye:

- **How often do you have to get up from your chair to retrieve things that are out of reach?**
- **Is there space and absence of clutter on your desktop to allow you to work comfortably and without distraction?**
- **Are your computer keyboard and monitor positioned so that you can use them comfortably and without undue fatigue?**
- **Is there space adjacent to your computer workstation for any papers you need while you are working at it?**
- **Are your cupboards, drawers and bookcases crammed with items you don't need?**
- **Is your storage equipment appropriate for the items you need to keep in it?**

- Do you regularly have to spend time searching for things?
- Is your office furniture best positioned for your different needs – working at your desk, using the computer, meeting with colleagues or customers?

There is no standard recipe for organising your work space – what feels comfortable to you may not to somebody else – but there are some general principles that you should consider in arriving at the best arrangement for you.

Think about ergonomics

Ergonomics is the process of designing machines, work methods and environments to take into account the safety, comfort and productivity of human users. It might sound rather grand when applied to the business of organising your work space, but there is no doubt that the choice and positioning of furniture, equipment, reference material and accessories can have a major impact on the way you work.

Furniture

Desks

Your desk needs sufficient clear space for you to be able to work comfortably and without distraction. We will come onto clearing the clutter a little later. If you have to divide your time between computer and paperwork, consider a modern wrap-around style which allows you to move between a traditional desktop and computer workstation without getting up. If you have any choice in the matter, go for a desk with adjustable height settings. Consider how the desk is placed in relation to your office space as a whole. Positioning your desk so that it forms a barrier between you and any visitor creates psychological distance. This may be the effect you want to create, but think

about moving it if you want to give a more accessible impression.
A desk which faces a wall may offer access to handy space for
shelves, pinboards, etc. For those working in an open-plan office,
facing a wall or screen serves to minimise distractions and casual
interruptions.

Chairs

Most modern office chairs are designed with castors and
swivel action, allowing you to move easily to different parts of
your workstation, and providing good back support to prevent
fatigue. Reject those which are a triumph of ostentation over
ergonomics, and signal more about your position in the
organisation than your productivity.

There is no such thing as an ideal chair for everybody, but
there are certain features you should look for:

- adjustable seat height;
- a backrest which is adjustable both vertically and in a
  forward–backward direction;
- seat depth which is sufficient if you are tall but not too
  great if you are short;
- adequate stability;
- castors, if required, which are appropriate for the type
  of flooring in your office.

Other equipment

It is a good idea to review from time to time the locations of
those accessories and items of equipment you use regularly. They
should be immediately to hand when you need them. If you have
shelves above your desk, it should be possible to reach the items
on the lowest one without standing up. Avoid placing items you
use frequently – telephone, printer, reference books – in
positions where you will need to stretch or twist in order to use
them. Have an eye to the changing nature of your job. It's quite
often the case that we leave reference books or items of
equipment in easily accessible places long after they have ceased

to be vital parts of our daily routine, while other things that have assumed greater importance are left out of reach. As little as 20 minutes spent reorganising your immediate workspace can pay productivity dividends.

Lighting

Many of the lighting problems in modern offices are associated with computer use, but it is important to have the right sort of lighting conditions for other activities too. Diffusers on overhead lights and the use of desk lamps can help to provide more comfortable conditions for reading and working with printed material.

Use of the computer

If your activities involve sustained computer use, taking some simple steps can enhance your productivity, increase your comfort and protect against injury and fatigue.

Here is a basic checklist to follow:

- **The normal recommendation is for the top of the monitor screen to be at eye level, although experts point out that this is the highest it should be, and maintain that for some users a slightly lower monitor proves more comfortable for the eyes and neck.**
- **Sit with a comfortable and balanced posture, paying particular attention to the position of your neck, spine, elbows, wrists, thighs and feet.**
- **Don't remain in one position for lengthy periods.**
- **Keep the forearms, wrists and hands in a straight line and don't rest them on sharp edges. Don't hit the keyboard too hard.**
- **The keyboard should be at the same angle as the forearms.**
- **Take frequent breaks from computer activity. Experts suggest 5 to 10 minutes every hour.**

- Reading paper documents generally requires better illumination than reading computer screens. If you are working with paper and computer simultaneously, an adjustable desk light can provide additional light on the paper without casting a glare on the computer screen.
- A copy holder, either of the free-standing variety or the type that fixes to the side of your monitor, will make it easier for you to view any notes or documents you are using while working on the computer. If you are able to keep your paper copy at roughly the same distance from your eyes as the computer screen, it saves your eyes having to refocus every time you look from one to the other.

Reading from computer screens

For a number of years now it has been accepted that reading from a screen is generally less efficient and more wearing than reading from the printed page. Studies in the past have shown that we are on average 25 per cent slower when reading from a monitor and have greater difficulty understanding what we read. When proofing documents on-screen there is an acknowledged tendency to miss errors that would be readily spotted on paper. Such difficulties with on-screen reading have been attributed to the lower resolution at which monitors display text, and the fact that on-screen fonts tend to have a more ragged edge than printed ones, which the brain finds more difficult to interpret. It's reasonable to assume though, that the considerable advances in monitor size and resolution in recent years, and the efforts that have been made to design fonts specifically for on-screen reading should have reduced the deficiency. However, at the time of writing (2009) there appears to be little new research to indicate whether the gap between page and screen is narrowing. A study from the University of Utah has found that when carrying out tasks such as editing documents and copying numbers between spreadsheets, users are significantly faster when operating on a

24 inch monitor as opposed to an 18 inch one, but this may not simply be an issue of reading speed. A large monitor, with its ability to display two windows side by side, is clearly more suited to jobs that involve moving data between files.

It's possible too that the difficulties we experience when reading from computer screens are not entirely physical ones. We tend to give on-screen text a more cursory treatment, and one psychological factor behind this is frequently the reader's awareness that an internet page is perhaps one of millions competing for his or her attention. The consequent sense of not knowing whether this is the page offering the 'best' information makes for a tendency to flit through a document rather than committing to it.

Whatever the mix of physical and psychological factors that may be limiting your on-screen reading productivity, there are some simple things you can do to minimise them:

1. Choose the best-quality monitor you can, and set your screen display to the highest available resolution.
2. Position monitors so that light is not reflected off them. Take care also that you are not having to deal with extremes of contrast – a monitor placed in front of a window, where the sunlight outside contrasts heavily with the screen, can be very hard on the eyes. Use window blinds and diffusers on overhead lighting to counteract these problems.
3. Adjust the contrast and brightness on your computer screen to a comfortable level.
4. Rest your eyes every 10 or 15 minutes by closing them momentarily, gazing at a distant object and blinking frequently.
5. Clean the computer screen regularly.
6. Don't get too close to the screen. It tends to strain both your eyes and neck. Standard reading glasses used for computer work may be the culprit. You may need glasses with a prescription that allows you to focus at the right distance.

7. Make full use of the advantages that computers have over the printed page. Rather than scrolling through a lengthy document, use the 'find' facility to locate key information quickly, and use embedded links to follow up other valuable references.
8. Choose the 'reading layout' if available on your word processor when you wish to read or proof documents. The display and fonts are specially designed for easier screen reading.
9. Search engines such as Google will often present you with a choice of format – pdf or html. The Adobe pdf format is generally the more readable as it captures text and graphics exactly as they were on the printed page. It may also incorporate additional help in navigating your way through lengthy documents.

Tackle disorganised work space

Disorganised work space is a potent source of wasted time and unnecessary stress. Tackling it is a tangible commitment to a more effective way of working. The area on and around your desk is the most important part of your working environment, and you might be tempted to tackle it first. But I suggest that you begin by clearing cupboards and drawers, in order to free up space to accommodate items that are cluttering your immediate desk area.

Organising cupboards, drawers and bookcases

These are all handy hiding places for things you don't need. Start by looking at the cupboards furthest away from your desk – they are likely to have the greatest proportion of redundant material, untouched by previous purges – and move inwards towards your desk. That way you will always have space to house items that are currently jamming up more immediate working areas. Clear out the junk ruthlessly. If there are items that really cannot be discarded, but hardly ever need to be looked at, put them in archive boxes or another long-term storage facility. Remember to take a note of the box contents and file it where you will be able to find it.

Work through all your cupboards and drawers, discarding junk, grouping like items together and making sure that items such as box files are clearly labelled. With bookcases it helps to take everything out before rearranging according to subject matter. The fact that books come in stubbornly different sizes means that you won't be able to achieve perfect organisation, and you shouldn't waste time trying. All you are attempting to do is organise material so that you can quickly put your hand on it when the need arises.

Organising your desk space

I used to pretend that I could work well with a cluttered desk. Despite the various piles of paper, at times threatening to engulf the workspace, I claimed that I could easily put my hand on any document I needed and that shifting my attention from one task to another kept me sharp throughout my working day. It was nonsense, of course. Superfluous papers are a distraction from the job in hand in much the same way as interruptions and phone calls. It is all too easy to flit around a crowded desk, pecking at tasks rather than devoting the concentrated effort needed to complete them. The presence of a multiplicity of documents is also an excuse for procrastination. When you are struggling with one task, it's the most simple thing in the world to shift your energy and attention to another, seemingly more straightforward chore which beckons from the top of a nearby pile.

Searching can waste considerable amounts of time and throw up further distractions. Just consider the number of times you need to root through the piles when a request or phone call summons the presence of a particular piece of paper. Surveys have suggested that 15 minutes a day is a fairly conservative estimate. It doesn't sound much, does it? But when you consider that 15 minutes a day is equal to a week and a half out of every year, the waste of your time is much more apparent. What could you do with that time? If you are disorganised to the extent that you spend 30 minutes a day searching for things, then the reward for greater discipline could be almost three weeks of additional productive activity.

Desktop disorganisation also destroys your ability to set priorities. Within the same pile there are likely to be scribbled notes, half-drafted reports, important letters and complete junk. All share a common fate – their importance is only considered when they come to the top of the pile or force themselves on your consciousness in the course of a search for something else.

And then there is the sheer inefficiency of it all. When you start a new task you have to clear some working space, pushing previously incomplete activity into yet higher piles. The same items pass through your hands numerous times, surfacing and resurfacing from the confusion of papers. You waste energy on things that should have been discarded the very first time you saw them. You miss deadlines because the papers that would remind you of them are buried under heaps of other stuff. You even find yourself sorting through the waste paper basket for that important piece of information you remember scribbling on a scrap of paper, which might have been the one which made no sense to you when you picked it out of the pile this morning.

Finally there is the stress. All the time that your untackled paperwork is an amorphous mass, it represents a potent source of disquiet. You are not entirely sure what lurks within those piles and they remain an ever-present reminder of your failure to get on top of your job. Very often the awareness of tasks to be done is more stressful than actually doing them.

So are you convinced? Sure. All that remains now is to do something about it. Simplicity has to be the keynote of your desk organisation. One of everything is a good place to start – one in tray, one out tray, one diary, one notebook. Think about whether you need personal clutter around your desktop. You may want to keep the odd photo or memento but there should be no sense in which personal reminders impose on your ability to work effectively. Accessories and equipment on your desktop should consist of items that you use daily. Other things may be kept close to hand but away from your main working surface. Give yourself plenty of space to work. There is a psychological advantage to the absence of clutter as well as a physical one.

You may need to overcome a mental hurdle in clearing your desk. There is a tendency to associate the crowded desk with a busy owner, and we like to think of ourselves as busy. Remember, however, that one can be busy but incompetent and unproductive. Let the results of your activities speak for you rather than the appearance of your desk. Once you are clear about what has a place on your desk, you are ready to tackle the piles.

Get rid of the piles

The prospect of tackling the piles of paper which have built up on your desk and around your office may be intimidating, but by setting aside some time for a disciplined blitz, you can get rid of them and lift the mental weight of their presence. In addition to items which need action on your part or should be directed to others, it is likely that your paper piles will consist of documents (reports, periodicals, etc) which you have put aside to be read later, items which have not made it to the filing cabinet, and things which you were not sure what to do with.

Your objective is to get through the paper piles; you must not let yourself become bogged down. So, be prepared to attack the offending heaps and deal quickly and decisively with their contents (Figure 6.1, overleaf):

- **Earmark four empty folders, filing trays or baskets and mark them: Deal with, Distribute, Read, File.**
  Make sure you have sufficient sturdy plastic bin bags for the most important category – the discard pile.

- **Approach the task with the view that the majority of items are destined for the bin.**

Whatever relevance they had when they joined the pile is likely to have diminished. Don't repeat previous indecisiveness. If in doubt, throw it out.

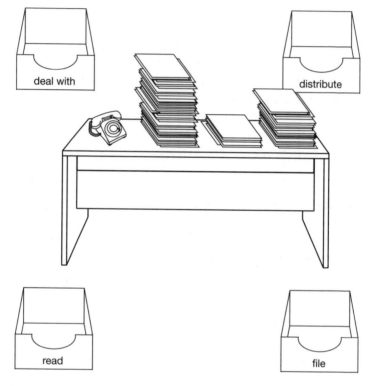

Figure 6.1   Get rid of the piles

- **Don't waste time reading items.**

Skim them to the point of determining whether they are needed and if so put them in the relevant tray or basket.

- **Don't file or act upon things as you go; you will become bogged down and distracted.**

By all means mark items to assist your actions and filing later, but keep to your main objective – to blast through the pile.

- **Zip through magazines and periodicals.**
Tear out the pages containing articles you wish to keep and throwing the rest away. Don't stop to read any of them at this stage.
  - **When you have worked your way through the piles, turn your attention to the four trays.**
Schedule time to deal with the reading and filing tasks, and use a 'bring forward' system with a concertina file or reminders in your PIM to determine when the 'deal with' items will be actioned.

Tackled in this way, a fearsome chore can become a real stress buster.

Keeping your work space organised

OK, so you've managed to sort the contents of your office. The things you use regularly are close at hand, you have ditched the junk and cleared the piles. How do you keep it that way?

The answer is, I'm afraid, a boring one. It has a lot to do with developing positive work habits:

- **Move paperwork quickly in line with the five Ds outlined in Chapter 4.**
- **If in doubt throw it out!**
- **Don't use your desk as filing space – use project folders or 'bring forward' files for work in progress (see Chapter 7).**
- **Keep your equipment needs under review. Are the items you use regularly still in the most accessible places?**
- **Don't transfer piles of paper on your desk to piles of paper in other parts of the office.**
- **Try to file on a daily basis. When you remove items from your filing cabinets, make a practice of re-filing them as soon as possible.**

Clear clutter at home

Everything that has been written about organising your workspace applies just as much to your home. If you're living amid clutter it will affect your ability to do the things you want to do, both in work and leisure terms. And a cluttered home is even more common than a cluttered workspace – we have a psychological attachment to many of the things that we bring into our homes and can display a surprising degree of reluctance to discard items that have long since outlived their usefulness. What's more, around the home there tend to be lots more places where clutter can accumulate.

Clutter isn't just unsightly, it's a potent source of wasted time. The list of things we spend time looking for around the home can be quite lengthy: tools, utensils, stationery items, keys, books and magazines, clothes and shoes, letters, bills and receipts, tapes and CDs, directories and address books. You may even think of some additional categories that apply in your own case. Take a moment to ask yourself what are the main items you spend time looking for and what are the reasons you regularly misplace them. Could it be because they don't have habitual storage locations to which they are routinely replaced? Or is it because the items concerned are simply overwhelmed among lots of other clutter that should have been discarded? You might like to conduct an audit of your own situation over a period of days as a way of galvanising yourself into action.

So, how do you bring some organisation into your home space to accompany the steps you have taken in your work area?

- **You can start with a similar sort of blitz to the one I described earlier in relation to office workspace, but don't try to tackle the whole house at once.**
Take it a room at a time. Once again separate items into four categories, but this time make them: items to keep, items to store, items to donate to the charity shop and items to ditch. Be

particularly ruthless with the 'items to store' category. Rather like paperwork filing, you can be pretty sure that most of the things you pile into the loft will never be needed again.

- **Once you have decided what you are going to keep, make sure there is a suitable home for everything.**
Magazines that go back into a pile will start the clutter cycle all over again. Work hard over the next three or four weeks at returning items to their proper place until you have built up a regular habit. While you're achieving this, it's a good idea to have a mini purge at the end of each day, putting things away.

- **Just as with your workspace, take care to house the things you use frequently in the most accessible locations.**
- **Ensure that you have suitable storage for the things you are going to keep.**
A filing system that you habitually maintain for essential paperwork is often just as much a priority in the home as it is in the office. Stackable storage boxes can be useful for those objects that aren't readily housed in drawers or cupboards. Just make sure that you label them appropriately and keep like items together, so that you don't have to rummage through the lot whenever you want a single item.

- **In working to build up an organised habit, pay particular attention to the places where things tend to accumulate – the kitchen table, for example, or by the front door.**
- **Make a rule that for every new item of furniture or equipment you acquire, you will get rid of something.**
- **With items that you have in multiple numbers, ask yourself seriously how many you really need, and get rid of those surplus to requirements.**

Summary

The key aspects of organising your space are:

- arranging your furniture and equipment to maximise safety, comfort and productivity;
- freeing up time and space by reorganising your desk and storage space;
- reducing stress by eliminating stacks of paper around your office;
- tackling the clutter around your home.

7

Organise filing systems

Not all that many years ago, a chapter such as this would have been all about the physical storage of documents. Today, we need to take account of the sheer amount of information that never finds its way into print – e-mails, web pages, shared electronic files – as well as the options for electronic storage of paper documents, and we will do so later in the chapter.

Nevertheless, it's with traditional manual storage that we will start. Regardless of how technically geared up you are, it is likely that there will continue to be documents you will keep in paper form. Original hard copy may be required for legal or taxation reasons, or it may be simply that some items would be too much of a hassle to store electronically.

Surveys have consistently shown that filing is the organisational chore that people hate the most, and our very loathing of it may mean that we give insufficient attention to doing it well. The only reason for putting a document into a file is so that you can find it again, and the only reason you might want to do that is to help you fulfil some aspect of your future work.

Up to 85 per cent of the material stored in the average filing cabinet is never referred to again. That means, for every five documents painstakingly categorised, punched and filed, possibly just one will be needed in the future. And the chances are that the one that is needed will prove frustratingly difficult to locate. It's a case of the 85 per cent you don't need getting in the way of the 15 per cent that you do.

You can never predict with certainty those documents you will need again. Some things do need to be stored on a 'just in case' basis, but you can drastically cut down on the chore of filing and failure to find the documents you need by more confident use of the 'discard' option when you first receive material. Filing is not a matter of getting a document off your desk when you're frightened to throw it away, but are not sure what else to do with it. A document should only make it to the filing cabinet when it cannot be readily accessed elsewhere and there is a reasonable chance that it will be needed again in the future.

If you can step away from a defensive filing mentality – better save it, just in case – to an attacking frame of mind, then you have much more chance of getting yourself a lean, mean filing system that works for you. For every document you consider filing, ask yourself 'What use will this document be to me in the future?' If you don't get a convincing answer, ditch it.

In addition to defensive filing, there are a number of other common document storage problems. How many of the following apply to you:

- **inappropriately located information?**
- **no structure to the filing system?**
- **a structure which hasn't been kept to?**
- **insufficient thought given to the appropriate grouping of items to allow for easy retrieval?**
- **failure to weed out obsolete material?**
- **forgetting what files you already have and setting up folders which duplicate existing categories of information?**
- **filing material that is easily accessible elsewhere?**
- **setting up too many categories within a system so that it becomes unmanageable?**

- use of inappropriate storage equipment for particular types of material (eg suspended files straining to hold weighty reports and periodicals)?
- time spent searching for things which have been misfiled?
- indecision about where to put things?
- missing files that have been 'borrowed' by a person or persons unknown?

Locate information appropriately

Your choice of location and storage medium should take account of the frequency with which you may need to consult files.

Current projects and activities

These are files which you may need to consult several times in the course of a day and so should be kept either in desk filing drawers or in a filing cart immediately next to your desk. As well as files for individual projects or assignments in progress, you may want to earmark a file each for correspondence pending, reading and meetings. They can help you to avoid the tendency to put things back into your in tray or to create piles on your desk. If you choose this approach, you need to take care that these files don't become general dumping areas. 'To read' files are particularly prone to this. General files may also result in date-related information being overlooked – preparatory reading for a meeting, for example, or a letter which needs to be answered by a particular date. Use a concertina file with a 'bring forward' system (see page 66) to overcome this problem.

Main reference files

Your main filing system is for the things you need to refer to from time to time. Material from the current projects and activities category will find its way there provided it is worth keeping. Don't simply transfer current project files to your main filing cabinet when the project is completed. Very often they will be cluttered with working papers and rough drafts that are of no further significance. Ruthlessly weed out the junk if you want to be able to lay your hands on the important stuff.

Setting up your filing system

First decide on broad divisions in which you want to group your files. These will clearly depend on the nature of your work, but examples of category titles might include: clients, staff, projects and administration. You might like to consider colour coding files within each category, so that when seeking a file you can quickly go to the right part of the cabinet. This is particularly useful when you are using a lateral filing system rather than a drawer filing cabinet. Alphabetical order is normally the most convenient arrangement for individual files within a category.

In deciding the titles for individual files, choose the broadest possible description consistent with manageability. You will want to avoid the need to split overlarge files within a short time and, equally, will not want to find yourself with lots of files each containing just a few documents. Neither is conducive to easy retrieval, which is the sole reason you are engaged in the task. If your file headings are too broad, then you might as well leave the documents in piles. Don't try to predict all the files you may need in the future – you'll end up with some empty folders if you do – but remember that your system needs the capacity to expand rationally, so allow space within files and sections for it to do so. Keep titles short and simple, and try to avoid descriptions that are vague or woolly. Miscellaneous files are notorious black holes.

Choose storage which is appropriate for the material. Use magazine files or box files rather than hanging folders for bulky reports and periodicals. Consider whether you need to store complete copies of magazines and periodicals. Cuttings take up far less room and it is much easier to find the item you want.

Filing documents

If you are following the paper handling procedures recommended in Chapter 4, you will already have weeded out that which isn't worth keeping. Here are some additional pointers to ensure that your paper storage is as effectively managed as possible:

1. Make a note indicating the intended destination file at the top of any document you have decided to file. This prevents you having to reread and decide on destination when you actually come to file the document.

2. If you are uncertain about where to put an item, think about the most likely context in which you are liable to require it in the future.

3. Keep a list of your files handy to help refresh your memory when deciding where to file an item, and to avoid opening new files which overlap with those that already exist.

4. Don't file hard copy of information already stored on computer. Ensure a sensible directory structure for your computer files with reliable back-up. It is quicker to do, easier to find and amend, and takes up less room.

5. Don't file material which is readily available from other sources such as the originator of the document, central archives, internet reference sources.

6. Build up a filing habit. Spending a little time regularly is much less of a chore than trying to wade through a large pile of documents for filing. Try to file daily if possible.

7. If you are tempted to file an item you haven't been bothered to read, ask yourself a very serious 'Why?'

8. If missing files are a problem in your office, a simple tracking system can be introduced. Keep some A4 cards by the filing cabinets, each divided into three columns: Name, Location, Date. Anybody borrowing a file enters their details on the card and places it in the appropriate empty file pocket.

Pruning and weeding your files

Without regular attention, files can rapidly get out of hand. The storage life of material varies hugely according to the nature of the information. Some items become redundant in a matter of weeks, while others need to be kept for years. Weeding out what needs to be discarded or archived can be daunting. If you are working with a file and notice that it contains obsolete information, weed it out there and then, but don't let yourself be distracted from your current task into a lengthy sorting process.

Try to schedule a regular file overhaul. You may opt either for 'big bang' or for 'little and often'. The former is a trawl through all your files, say, every three months. The latter might mean spending five or ten minutes sorting a couple of files at the end of each day. Both have drawbacks. If you're overloaded, and who isn't these days, the big bang tends to get postponed indefinitely until a very serious problem builds up. Little and often requires some attention to building up a habit.

However you set about the task, you need to be ruthless with the rubbish and not to allow yourself to become bogged down in spin-off tasks. If there are items which have been misplaced, or one file needs to be merged with another, just put the items where they need to go, and resist the temptation to sort the destination file unless it is one you have already dealt with. Its turn will come in due course.

Electronic filing of paper documents

Storing documents electronically has the advantage of saving much of the time and space occupied by traditional filing methods, as well as greatly facilitating the sharing of data and retrieval of information. The ever-increasing capacity and tumbling cost of the required hardware mean that an electronic filing system is within the scope of any PC user. All that is needed is a scanner, appropriate software and a storage device such as a writable CD/DVD or additional hard drive. If you are going to be processing a large number of documents, it helps for the scanner to have an automatic sheet feeder. The necessary software to scan and save your documents will generally come bundled with the scanner, but a relatively inexpensive upgrade or purchase of a leading OCR package such as OmniPage will generally add much greater sophistication and ease of use. Such software will allow you to scan documents directly into Word or Excel, as well as converting documents to the most convenient format for electronic storage – pdf files. These save documents in relatively compact files with all the formatting, text and graphics exactly as they appeared in the original. Searchable pdf files can be indexed by any word in the text and read by anyone who has the free Adobe Reader software on their computer. The format has become a worldwide standard for sharing documents.

Managing your scanned documents

There are a number of software products that aim to help you manage and retrieve electronically filed documents. Some such as PaperPort by Nuance (www.nuance.com) provide powerful search and retrieval facilities in addition to sophisticated assistance with the process of scanning, conversion into searchable pdf files, annotation where required and organisation into easily manageable folders. For those whose needs are for indexing and retrieval alone, there are competent desktop search tools to locate files of all types. Some of these operate on a subscription basis, while others can be downloaded free of charge. They vary in their degree of sophistication. Some, for example, will search network drives as well as the immediate machine. Free of charge front runners at the time of writing include Copernic, Google Desktop and Microsoft Windows

Desktop Search. Google Desktop is typical in that it works quietly in the background while your computer is idle, indexing all those files containing information you might wish to retrieve (you can choose the types of files you want included). The software then offers a very rapid search facility in the familiar Google style, which will find any document that matches your chosen search words or phrases. You should be aware that if your computer is not particularly fast, use of a desktop search tool may slow it down further.

Electronic tracking of paper files

If the prospect of converting the majority of your files to electronic storage is just too daunting, or you have a substantial filing system that just has to remain in a paper form, you could possibly adopt the halfway house of using electronic means to track your paper files. Several companies offer software that aims to assist in manual filing and make it a simple matter to locate items needed. Some of these make use of sophisticated tools like barcodes and are only suitable for adoption on an organisation-wide basis. However, there are a few relatively inexpensive packages that may meet the needs of the individual or small business. One such is Paper Tiger (www.thepapertiger.com). This offers a searchable database that allows you to designate different locations for information – reference files, document boxes, notebooks, etc – and instead of labelling each file pocket or document box with its contents, to use a simple ascending sequence of numbers. Keywords are entered against numbered locations and a rapid search facility will immediately reveal the whereabouts of any item. The software removes the bother of labelling files, and there is less need for a rigid concern about categorising and keeping like items together. Another package, DocsToBox (www.docstobox.com) offers a similar facility in respect of documents that have been archived.

Organising computer files

You might feel that, with all the sophisticated file management and search tools now available, attention to organising your computer files is unnecessary, but I would still strongly advocate a simple and logical grouping of material into folders and sub-folders. It takes very little time to do, it makes tasks like archiving more straightforward, and there will be many occasions when it is quicker to go to a sub-folder where you know you can locate a file than to attempt recall of a name or keyword in order to run a search.

Needless to say, you should start by ensuring that the files you have created are separate from any program files on your computer. Using the 'Documents' facility provided by your operating system (My Documents in Windows XP and earlier) makes it easier to locate them, to back them up and to prevent accidental erasure.

I suggest that you then decide what will be your main current storage directory. My preferred way of working is to create a new main folder for word processed and spreadsheet documents each year, while maintaining separate directories for other types of files. This allows for easy archiving and prevents subdirectories of routine documents getting out of hand. However, depending upon the nature and volume of your work there may be other approaches that work better for you. Within your main directory set up subfolders for the different categories of activity and types of routine document you create. Produce additional subfolders for any major projects that will require significant groupings of documents.

Once you have arrived at the most logical grouping of documents to meet your needs, it's important to stick to the system. If you find yourself with an overly large number of subfolders within a folder, you may need to consider splitting it or indexing of subfolders in some way.

Next, inform your computer applications where to put things. When you click on the 'Open' or 'Save' command, you want the computer to go to your current main storage directory and you may need to change the existing settings so that it does so. Such changes are generally made by clicking on the 'Options' or 'Preferences' command within your application's 'Tools' menu.

Choosing file names

It's all about simplicity and accessibility once again. It greatly helps to have filenames that mean something to you when you seek them out. You don't want the irritation and wasted time of opening a file only to find that it is not what you thought it was. If your software automatically offers a filename based on the headings used for the document this may be adequate, but frequently such names are overly lengthy and you should take care if you're producing a number of documents that have similar headings. Documents such as letters or minutes may be best saved with a name and date (eg Bloggs 151209 or Safety 300609) so that other documents relating to the same person or meeting can be easily identified.

Securing your information

Failure to organise the security of your information adequately may leave you with a loss of precious data, time-consuming recovery tasks and embarrassment or worse as far as your employers or clients are concerned. As with most other organisational issues, it's a matter of deciding on your objectives, putting measures in place to achieve them, and building regular habits in order to maintain them.

The security issues most likely to concern you are:

- **back up of computer data;**
- **selection and maintenance of passwords;**
- **protection from malicious attack;**
- **physical security of equipment and data;**
- **security of paper-based information.**

Backup

Few office experiences can be more stressful than the complete loss of days, weeks or months of work through inadequate attention to backup. Seldom is it wholly impossible to recover lost information but, depending on the nature of the data loss, recovery may be time-consuming or expensive.

What do you back up?

It's quite feasible to back up your entire system, and indeed you can make this an automatic process, but you may decide that isn't necessary. If a crash occurs, applications can be reinstalled, although this can be a time-consuming process. The files you have created yourself are the ones you absolutely must back up, and you will save yourself an awful lot of hassle if you also back up the settings for the operating system and main applications. There are dozens of applications that can help make backup a simple, reliable and, if you wish, automatic procedure. Some are included with well-known utility suites, while others are stand-alone packages.

Where to back up

There are now a host of inexpensive backup media – additional hard drives, CD and DVD, flash drives, network drives and online storage facilities. The most important consideration is that you should not be backing up onto the same hard drive that contains your original files and, to guard against loss of data through theft or fire, the place where you store your back up information should be separate from your PC.

Passwords

Many of us are guilty of laxity as far as passwords are concerned. We choose words that we will remember easily, but which may be just as easily guessed by others. We use the same password in multiple situations, and we fail to change them when there is a chance that they might have become compromised.

A poorly selected password is almost as bad as no password at all. You should avoid drawing them from personal information, which can be easily guessed by people who have access to your details, and it is also wise to steer clear of standard dictionary words. The best passwords are those which mix numbers, upper and lower case letters and special characters in a manner that is unpredictable for anybody trying to access them. Of course, these are the most difficult passwords to remember, and you may wish to use mnemonics to help you remember them. Alternatively, you could purchase a password manager. These computer applications routinely generate high quality passwords, store them in an encrypted form, and may have an auto-insert facility to call them up when needed for online activity. Some password managers are better and more secure than others, so do check reviews before purchasing.

If you really have no alternative but to write passwords down, then at least keep them in a secure place and disguise the actual passwords in such a way that they will mean something to you but will be unintelligible to anybody else.

Physical security of equipment and data

These days we have access to so many reliable, cheap and versatile data storage devices that it's easy to lose track of the locations where information is held. With laptops, DVDs, portable hard drives, data sticks and smartphones in abundance, you need to be organised if you are to stay in control. Whilst the effect of losing a data storage device might not be as dramatic for you as it has been in some of the cases that have hit the headlines in recent years, it is likely at the very least to cause some inconvenience, embarrassment and wastage of time. Here are a few measures you might consider to protect yourself:

- Limit the number of storage devices you use – you are asking for trouble if you carry multiple memory sticks around.
- If you are using a portable device to transfer information between computers, make a habit of deleting the data it contains once the transfer is complete.
- Destroy CD or DVD data discs as soon as they have fulfilled their purpose, and ensure that discarded hard drives are put beyond use.
- Use specialist software to permanently and securely delete sensitive or confidential information that is no longer needed.
- Protect your laptops and phones with decent passwords. Laptops are often configured to connect automatically to your home or workplace network, and leaving them insecure risks not only the data held on the laptop itself, but may also leave the network wide open.

Another problem arising from the proliferation of portable storage devices is failure to keep track of the location that holds the latest version of a file you may be working on. You may find yourself losing the results of hours of work if you're not careful. Once again it's a matter of building disciplined habits. Be clear which of your devices you will use to store master copies of files, and ensure that other machines are routinely synchronised with it.

Protection from malicious attack

There are numerous packages available to protect your computer from internet-based attacks. Some quite competent applications even come free of charge. Read reviews in the computer press to find the most suitable applications to suit your needs. At the very least you should have a firewall in place, together with some anti-virus and anti-spyware software. Many of the commercial packages will also give you added security such as identity protection and e-mail security. But needless to say, you shouldn't just set up the protection and forget about it. New threats are constantly emerging, so it's important to initiate regular scans and updates.

Security of paper-based information

By now most people are aware that personal information contained in discarded documents may be used in the course of identity theft. It makes sense to have decent measures in place for the disposal of any paperwork containing your own details and, of course, you have a legal duty to deal appropriately with personal or sensitive information concerning others. Shredders are cheap enough and easy to use; it's really a matter of ensuring that you use them routinely. If you're buying a shredder for a home office setup, get the crosscut variety. They do a much better job of rendering a document unreadable than do the cheaper strip cut shredders.

Summary

Effective storage of information requires:

- clarity about what is and is not worth filing;
- a simple and logical structure that is routinely adhered to;
- regular pruning of redundant material;
- attention to the security of your data.

8

Use technology to assist

Technology may be both an aid to organisation and a factor leading to greater disorganisation. Technologically assisted generation and communication of information has led to a huge increase in the volume of information in daily circulation, and far from achieving the paperless office envisaged in the early 1980s, ever-larger quantities of paper are being produced, handled and stored. Add to that the increasing use of e-mail and the biggest information repository of all, the internet, and you have a recipe for overload. But the tremendous capacity of technology to assist us in creating, communicating, manipulating and storing information also offers potential solutions to the problem. Your success in this will depend on judicious choice and effective use of the available tools.

Know when not to use technology

Information technology has become so all pervading that one may be tempted to use it for every information handling task.

This would be a mistake. There are occasions when the effort of using technology outweighs the advantage, or the medium is inappropriate:

- setting up a spreadsheet to produce a handful of one-off calculations that could be done quicker and just as reliably on a calculator;
- engaging in excessive internet research before embarking on a creative task, and finding yourself overwhelmed with other people's ideas before you have a chance to formulate your own;
- using e-mail, text messaging or instant messaging in unsuitable situations – for example, interactions requiring sensitivity or subtlety that call for face-to-face or, at the very least, telephone contact;
- using time and energy to learn a software package for a function that could be performed manually and has only marginal or occasional significance in your workload.

Choose appropriate software

Let genuine needs drive your software decisions. It is all too easy to be enticed by the productivity claims of a particular software package, and having acquired it, to look around for a task on which to use it. Using a product to meet an identified need is generally an effective way of learning it, but take care not to set yourself unrealistic timescales for achieving your targets with a new application.

Match the pay-off in terms of improved productivity against the investment of time to become proficient in the application. Even if a package looks straightforward, allow plenty of time to get to grips with it. There may be unexpected glitches to overcome.

The value of a particular package will vary from person to

person. It will be dependent on how much you have used other similar products, the way you like to work and the precise nature of your job. Use magazine reviews and recommendations to aid your decision, but recognise that only you can make an accurate assessment of whether an application is worth having.

If you are a computer novice

Computers are so ubiquitous these days that some publications appear to assume everybody is familiar with the basics. I'm conscious however that there are still many computer novices out there, some of whom will be included within my readership. You may not be entirely new to computers – possibly you have used a word processor to a limited degree and dabbled with e-mail and the internet – but you are perhaps unsure how to move on from there and harness the power of technology to assist your personal organisation.

The most common problems for new computer users are not knowing where to start, and fear of making disastrous mistakes. The first is a matter of taking one's courage in both hands and pitching in. To the novice, everything may seem daunting, but each step forward makes the next one less difficult. Many computer operations have the same basic format and there are a host of good tutorials available. Once you have mastered the basics, nothing can beat tackling a real project for reinforcing and progressing your learning.

Conquering fear of making mistakes starts with the understanding that there is almost nothing irretrievable you can do from the keyboard. Take care to save your work regularly and even seemingly catastrophic situations can be salvaged. It is helpful if there is somebody experienced to call upon when the unpredictable does happen, as it surely will from time to time. There is usually a simple and easily executed solution. If you don't have expert assistance, try to approach the difficulty methodically, making use of the troubleshooting section in your software manual or the help facility within the application.

Don't try to learn too much at once. Get to grips with one package before moving on to the next. The majority of software has very similar screen layout and commands. If you have mastered one package, you can easily transfer to the next your knowledge of the familiar features, and work to address those aspects that are different.

If you are an experienced computer user

Before embarking on a new application, try to arrive at a realistic assessment of the benefits set against the investment of time in learning to use it. One way to do this is to estimate a payback period. The questions to ask yourself are:

- **What will I use this package for?**
- **How much time per week do I currently spend doing these tasks?**
- **What are the weekly time savings I might reasonably expect once I am a competent user of the package?**
- **How many learning hours will it take for me to achieve reasonable competence?**

If you then divide the learning hours estimate by the figure for weekly time savings, you will arrive at an estimated payback period. For example, if it takes you 20 hours to learn a package that only saves you 30 minutes a week, the payback period will be 40 weeks. In other words, it will be almost a year before you derive any time saving. In this situation, there are likely to be other time investments which will produce more immediate rewards.

Deciding to upgrade

Whatever software package you choose, within a short time there is likely to be an upgrade version available, promising new features and greater effectiveness. Make the decision on whether to upgrade on the following basis:

Do I need the new features? Few of us use all the features of an application. New ones may sound attractive, but if they don't offer you significant benefits there is no point in acquiring them.

Are the advantages worth the learning investment? Most upgraded packages will be broadly similar to their predecessors, but sometimes there is a major redesign which will require you to 'relearn' the application. Against this, the improvements may only be marginal. An upgrade may, from time to time, introduce new bugs or frustrations, or may run more slowly on your computer.

Reviewing computer habits

The longer you have been using computers, the more likely it is that you will benefit from a review of your computer habits. Experienced users may find that they are locked into ways of doing things which were learnt when computers were slower and software less sophisticated; or that the trial and error way in which learning took place has bypassed important shortcuts. Half an hour revisiting the help file or manual of a software package or operating system may pay major dividends. Here are some of the things you might look for:

- **facilities which weren't present in earlier versions of applications or operating systems;**
- **keyboard shortcuts on commonly used commands;**
- **drag and drop procedures to replace lengthy operations;**
- **customisation of toolbars and menus.**

Useful tools

We have already given some consideration to the application of technology to assist personal organisation:

- **use of PDAs and PIMs in managing tasks and time (Chapter 2);**
- **effective management of e-mail (Chapter 4);**
- **electronic document management (Chapter 7).**

In the sections that follow, I shall briefly consider the organisational advantages offered by common office applications and look at various ways by which you might speed up the entry of data to your computer.

General office software

Word processors and spreadsheets

Word processors and spreadsheets have become such ubiquitous applications that we may be guilty of almost taking them for granted. But they are very powerful tools and most of us don't use them to anything like their full potential. We may tend to ignore some of the facilities that might save us time or enhance our personal organisation. For example, are you making use of the autotext and autofill tools for tasks that regularly require input of similar information? Could you benefit by using macros – mini programs that record your keystrokes and can help to simplify common procedures? Are you using AutoCorrect for all the words you commonly mistype, or painstakingly correcting them every time they come up? Do you have at your disposal templates that are appropriate for the major documents you need to produce, or are you wasting time producing standard materials from scratch? Are you using the proofing tools that are available to users of more recent applications and operating systems? The ability to have a document read out loud by a synthesised computer voice may be of particular use to those with visual impairment, but it can be a help to all users when checking documents – especially those that contain a lot of numbers.

Notes organisers

Personal Information Managers generally have space for notes which can be linked to contacts or tasks and, of course, you can use your word processor as a repository for all manner of notes. But neither of these is as flexible, comprehensive or accessible as a dedicated note organising package. Such applications provide you with a ready workspace where you can develop ideas, formulate objectives, build project outlines or pull together creative activity. They present you with a place to store and index the fruits of your research, including screenshots from websites, notes dropped in from other applications, and even bits of audio and video. They offer too a home for all those little bits of information that you want to keep but which don't fit with normal office applications, and which often end up on bits of paper floating around your desk. There are a number of note organising packages – some of them are designed for desktop operation, whereas others operate online. An online search will throw up a selection and, as ever, there are reviews and free trials to help you choose the package best suited to your needs. For my part, I'm a fan of Microsoft OneNote, which comes with some versions of Microsoft Office, or can be purchased as a standalone item. It's nicely intuitive with an attractive notebook style that can be easily customised, and it integrates well with other applications in the Microsoft Office suite. For example, it's possible simply to designate an item in OneNote as a 'to do' entry in Outlook, with a target date and associated reminder if required. Once marked as completed in Outlook, the item will be updated in OneNote too.

Presentation software

Applications such as Microsoft PowerPoint and Corel Presentations can not only speed up the process of preparing a presentation, but greatly enhance its impact. What's more, they are very easy packages to get to grips with. And therein lies the problem – their very ease of use tends to result in them being over-employed. In many work settings, a PowerPoint presentation has become the essential accompaniment whenever people get to their feet. It's a case of having the technology and then casting around for a job it can do rather than applying it judiciously to meet an identified need. Select the occasions that genuinely call for the use of presentation software and then use it well. A handful of vague and ill-designed slides thrown together to support a presentation seldom gives anything but the illusion of structure, and may not be worth the limited effort that has gone into producing them. Recognise that there are low-tech tools – flip charts and whiteboards – that will provide perfectly adequate support in many situations.

When you do decide to use presentation software, it helps greatly to have structured your thoughts before you start. A good presentation is one where the visual material supports the words, not the other way around. This may seem a pretty obvious statement, but it is often forgotten in the pressure to produce a zappy presentation. Make full use of templates to cut down the donkey work, and import other information from your word processor, spreadsheet or previous presentations rather than retyping it.

Desktop publishing software

DTP packages have become less prominent in general use as the sophistication of word processors has increased, but they still have a distinct edge on tasks that require attractive presentation of text and graphics in such things as brochures, newsletters and advertisements. At the top end of the range are the professional products such as Quark Xpress and Adobe InDesign, which are powerful and rather pricey. But there are well-respected and inexpensive DTP packages like Microsoft Publisher and Serif Page Plus, which combine ease of use with the capacity for sophisticated output. What many general users forget, however, is that design flair and skill are at least as important as the ability to use the software. Standard templates can help overcome our design deficiencies, but if you are tempted to use DTP software yourself to produce materials that need to have an impact, ask yourself honestly whether the product of your effort is likely to do justice to the organisation you represent and the investment of your time. Put a price on your time and set that against the cost of contracting the work out.

Rapid input of data

The extent to which you can speedily and reliably input data to a computer, from where it may be manipulated, edited, distributed and stored, is clearly a factor in how well you are able to manage information. If you are a two-finger typist, you may well despair of this aspect of your personal organisation. Let's spend a few moments looking at four applications designed to help you.

Voice recognition software

With a voice recognition package you can dictate material via a microphone or digital voice recorder, such as those found on PDAs, and the computer will convert your speech into text that can be fed directly into popular office programs such as Word. This type of software has been around for a number of years, but early packages conferred only limited benefits as they required the separate enunciation of each word in a manner that is difficult to achieve when speaking naturally. Increased processing power and ongoing software development mean that they now cope with normal speech, and producers claim up to 99 per cent accuracy with speeds up to 160 words per minute – much faster than even the most competent typist. But voice recognition is very complex technology seeking, as it does, to make sense of sounds delivered with a huge number of variables – diction, accent, modulation, emphasis – and users are by no means unanimous in their acceptance of it. In fact, it's fair to say that you either love or hate voice recognition.

When setting up a package, you have to be prepared to spend some time 'training' it to recognise your particular speech patterns and correcting a significant number of mistakes before the application becomes used to your voice. And you must continue a firm policy of correcting any errors in words or punctuation that crop up or, rather like an unruly pet, the software will repeat the misdemeanours and become less accurate. Correcting mistakes by voice can be an irritating chore. The inclination is simply to type in the correct word later, but that would perpetuate the error.

You should remember too that dictation is a skill in itself. Many of us have difficulty articulating our thoughts cogently and fluently in a manner that will work well on paper. If you find yourself constantly having to backtrack and amend sections of text, it can remove some of the time savings. And because voice recognition software works partly by identifying words in context, it prefers speech that is delivered in fluent sentences. Unexpected pauses and any humming and hawing can play havoc with its accuracy.

These reservations aside, there is most certainly a role for voice recognition, and I would particularly recommend it for those who have significant amounts of routine correspondence, or regularly need to transcribe rough notes to computer text. For my part, I have dabbled with voice recognition over the years, but it is only with the current generation of software, allied to fast processors and high quality Bluetooth wireless microphones and digital recorders, that I find it consistently generating the sort of results that lead me to use it as a reliable daily tool. I haven't yet managed to achieve accuracy at the levels indicated by the software producers, but for most routine text it delivers well into the 90per cent bracket. This probably rivals my typing accuracy, but at speeds way in excess of those I can achieve from the keyboard. The leading voice recognition product on the market is Dragon NaturallySpeaking distributed by Nuance (www.nuance.com), and there are also more limited voice recognition facilities in Windows operating systems from Vista onwards. To make use of such a package, your computer will need a reasonably fast processor and plenty of memory. Check the minimum specifications carefully before buying.

Handwriting recognition

Through years of practice, we have become adept at jotting down key points while simultaneously carrying out another action – taking part in a meeting, holding a telephone conversation or exploring a difficult idea – and there are many instances where the ability to make a handwritten note and have it converted into editable computer text is extremely useful. Handwriting recognition has been around for a number of years, but early incarnations required users to learn quite complex scripting techniques and were often not very accurate. The advent of faster processors, greater memory capacity and increased portability of devices has brought forward a number of hardware items that employ handwriting recognition and claim to make it easy and reliable – tablet PCs, digital pens, smartphones and PDAs. Nevertheless, handwriting recognition hasn't yet taken off in a big way, and for most purposes the keyboard is still quicker and more reliable. However, handwriting recognition may come into its own where the use of a keyboard is impractical – with smartphones for example, where the keyboard or virtual keyboard may be tiny, or in settings where use of a keyboard might be cumbersome, such as when taking notes in meetings or lectures. For such functions a tablet PC or digital pen may be a suitable input device. Users and reviewers are still divided on the value of handwriting recognition devices, and the extent to which they work for you will depend, to a degree, on the quality of your script. If, like me, you have handwriting that even you have difficulty deciphering, then your computer may not have an easy time of it.

Optical character recognition (OCR)

I have already referred to OCR in relation to the scanning and filing of documents, but it deserves a further mention here as a technique for rapidly inputting data without the need for retyping. The latest OCR software will read a printed page and import it to a standard office application – word processor, spreadsheet or presentation package – with all formatting intact. For example, a table of figures can be scanned and dropped straight into Excel with cells accurately filled, and ready to be manipulated in whatever way you require. Pro versions of OCR packages such as OmniPage and ABBYY FineReader also include useful tools to transfer documents between different formats and turn paper forms into electronic ones.

Keyboard training packages

Keyboards aren't about to disappear wholesale from our computers. Even those who use the above methods of data input extensively will generally find themselves working with a keyboard some of the time. If you are a two-finger typist, you may benefit from the increase in typing speed that follows from developing the use of all your fingers. There are a number of inexpensive keyboard trainers available on CD or online that take you through staged development and practice. It is not unreasonable to look for a doubling of your speed with 8 to 12 hours of work. If you have been typing with two fingers for a long time, then you might find it a little more difficult to make the change, but as a former two-finger typist of 30 years' standing I can testify that the change is possible with a little perseverance and makes a considerable difference to productivity.

Activity – ask yourself

Take this opportunity to review your current software use, and ask yourself whether there are changes you could make that might assist your personal organisation:

- What, if any, applications am I overusing or using inappropriately?
- With which applications that I currently use could I benefit from a review of my work habits in order to make better use of the available facilities and enhance my productivity?
- Are there applications that I do not currently use, but which I believe could make a significant difference to my productivity?
- Which of the above are likely to offer the best payback for the time I will spend learning new techniques or reviewing existing ones?

You might like to draw up a hit list in priority order – headed by those software-related tasks that offer the best payback – and incorporate it into your medium-term objectives and 'to do' list.

Organise internet research

The speed and ease with which you are able to access information on the world wide web can greatly assist with personal organisation, but the sheer volume of information available presents several difficulties:

- separating the information you need from the mass of less relevant data;

- deciding when to stop searching;
- avoiding the distraction presented by other interesting but irrelevant material;
- assessing the quality and reliability of information.

The internet is huge and seductively accessible. You are just a couple of mouse clicks away from billions of pages of information, and the temptation is toward excessive searching, out of fear of missing some vital piece of information tucked away in the vast unruly collection. But resist the urge to seek information perfection. Nowhere does the 80:20 rule apply more than on the internet (80 per cent of the results come from 20 per cent of the effort) and you can waste large amounts of time chasing a rapidly diminishing addition to useful data. Concentrate, instead, on precise and well-planned searches that will get you quickly to manageable quantities of quality information.

Research tools

There are two primary vehicles for locating information on the internet – directories and search engines. In the early days, these tended to be quite separate entities, but now most of the big names including Google and Yahoo offer both a directory and a search engine. The vastly increased power and scope of search engines has made them pre-eminent, but in deciding where to look for the information you require you should take account of both tools.

Internet directories

Internet directories are compiled by human beings, and index sites under subject headings with progressively more specialised sub-headings. Approaching an information-gathering task via an internet directory is rather like searching the catalogue of a library – fine for locating websites concerned with the subject you are interested in, but of limited value if what you are after is a specific reference that may be buried within a web page. You might want to approach your task via a directory if what you are looking for is a general overview within a topic area.

Search engines

Search engines are compiled and updated using 'web crawling' software, which trawls the world wide web looking for new pages and referencing the contents. This leads to much greater volumes of information than would be found in a directory and offers the ability to pull out a reference from deep within a web page. Locating the information you want is a matter of choosing the best combination of keywords. Google has far and away the largest search engine database, and that makes it the engine of choice for a great many users. But not even Google contains anywhere near the sum total of searchable material on the net, so there is certainly value in using other search engines if you don't find what you are seeking on Google.

Metasearch tools

These have no database of their own, but send the same enquiry to a variety of search engines, and may be useful if you are looking for a hard-to-find reference. One example is the quaintly named Dogpile (www.dogpile.com).

Searching tips

- **Take care in formulating your search request.**
  If you enter keywords that are too general, you risk being deluged with information.
  Search engines rank responses to queries, with those that most nearly meet the search criteria at the top of the list, but a vague enquiry may throw up thousands of responses with similar

rankings. Some lateral thinking may be necessary in choosing keywords likely to be in the material you are seeking.

- **Use inverted commas to enclose phrases when you wish the search engine to look for the complete phrase rather than the individual words that constitute it.**
- **Use the plus and minus symbols to narrow down your search.**

Preceding a search word with the minus symbol will exclude that word from the search and can be handy for stripping out references unrelated to the information you are seeking. The plus symbol indicates that you specifically want a word included, and is useful when you want the search engine to take account of small words that tend to be omitted from searches.

- **Every search engine has an 'advanced search' section.**

This will offer sophisticated filters that may be extremely useful when you are experiencing difficulty unearthing what you require through a standard search.

- **Don't let yourself be distracted by links to other interesting but irrelevant pages.**

If something attracts your interest, use the favourite places facility to store a record of the location so that you can return to it at a later date.

Assessing quality

Finding information quickly is all very well, but what about the quality and reliability of what you discover? Within the billions of pages of information on the world wide web there is an awful lot of garbage. Anybody who wishes can quite simply set up a website and present information in an apparently authoritative way. So how do you discriminate between the reliable and the less so? Here are some pointers that may help:

- *Is the site the work of a reputable body?*

Generally at the top of the list for reliability are: universities; national government information sites; local authorities; publicly funded bodies; known voluntary organisations; reputable companies; broadcasters; online versions of respected newspapers and periodicals.

- *Has the site been vetted in any way?*

There are some sites and directories that make a positive commitment to verifying the quality of the links they carry. One such is About (www.about.com). Each of the categories in its directory is controlled by a specialist in the subject matter concerned.

- *Is there anything else I can look for?*

If a search comes up with information held on a website with which you are unfamiliar, you may get some clues regarding its reliability by considering the following:

- – Are references given for any facts and figures, research or survey results?
- – How up to date is the information? Does the web page show a 'last reviewed' date?
- – Does the information have a clear target audience and obvious purpose?
- – What is the presentation like? A slap-happy approach to spelling, grammar or presentation may indicate a similar attitude towards the veracity of information.
- – Are there any clues to the status and expertise of the originator?
- – Does the site contain links to other clearly reputable websites?

- *Am I able to double-check the information?*

Similar information on different websites may offer some guide to validity, but take care. Identical or near-identical wording may indicate that it has simply been lifted from one site to the other.

- *Who uses the site?*

To discover who is responsible for a site, how much traffic it receives, how many other sites link to it and what other sites the people who visit it use, go to www.alexa.com and type or paste the address (URL) of the site you wish to know about into the Search box.

Organising the material you find

It's a simple enough matter to download pages for later reference or click on 'add to favourites' to save a link to an interesting or valuable site you may wish to visit again; but if you do a lot of internet research, you can quickly find your favourites list and the file location you use for downloads becoming cluttered and unwieldy. Use 'organize favorites' to set up appropriately labelled sub-folders within the favourites list and drop items from your list into the relevant folder. Similarly, create folders within your page download location that reflect either the subject matter of the downloaded pages or projects with which they are associated. Alternatively, you may wish to use a product such as PaperPort or OneNote (both mentioned earlier) which have a useful facility for capturing screenshots of webpages as well as filing and indexing them. Be judicious in what you choose to save – links are generally more valuable than downloaded pages that may rapidly become out of date. It is also a good idea to schedule a regular pruning session to clear out any downloads or favourites that have become redundant.

Summary

Modern information technology can be of considerable assistance in personal organisation provided it is used appropriately. You need to:

- recognise the tasks for which technology offers no appreciable advantage;
- select software to meet identified needs;
- balance potential time savings against the commitment of time to learn new software applications;
- review your computer habits periodically;
- adopt precise search techniques when seeking information on the internet;
- monitor the quality of information obtained;
- manage and organise any saved material.

9

Organise yourself at home and away

A study conducted in 2005 estimated that 5 million workers in the UK (almost 20 per cent of the workforce) spend some time working at home or on the move, and predicted a rapid rise in that figure over the ensuing decade as mobile technology continues to reduce the need for fixed work locations and rigid working hours. In the twenty-first century, no book on personal organisation would be complete without consideration of the special challenges that working from home or on the road presents.

Working from home

The range of working from home arrangements extends from those working full time in a self-employed capacity to those for whom an occasional bout of home working is an opportunity to escape the distractions of the office. But for all those who spend a significant amount of time working from home, the organisational advantages and difficulties are fairly similar.

Advantages:

- control over your own schedule;
- nobody looking over your shoulder;
- freedom from some workplace distractions;
- flexibility to slot leisure or personal activity into what would normally be considered working hours.

Difficulties:

- absence of normal workplace structures;
- lack of supporting colleagues – may need to juggle different roles;
- potential new distractions;
- absence of boundaries between work and home life;
- workspace limitations.

Clearly you will wish to maximise the advantages and minimise the disadvantages, and all the points made earlier in the book about managing time and understanding the way you work will be of significance. But there are additional issues specific to home working in respect of balance, focus and workspace organisation, which we might usefully look at now.

Balance

One of the biggest problems for home-based working is maintaining a balance between work and leisure. You are in control of your schedule, but unless you take care to set and maintain boundaries on your working day, you can find work beginning to invade all your waking hours and, without a degree of discipline, the work you do may not be very productive. With all the trappings of your home around you, there may be a tendency to flit between work tasks and leisure/family activity in a manner that reduces the effectiveness of your work and, because of guilt about neglected work tasks, does not permit full enjoyment of leisure activities.

To maintain a healthy and productive balance between work and leisure, build a structure to your working day. It may be helpful to see your day in terms of core time and flexible time using a broader approach to the common flexitime principle. The core time is that which will always be allocated to work or to family/leisure activity – no excuses, this time is sacrosanct. For example, you might decide that from 8.30 am until 1.30 pm every day is core working time and the period after 6.30 pm is core leisure time. The flexible time to make up your working week can move to accommodate a healthy leisure balance. One day might involve an early morning start, another some early evening work and a third might follow traditional office hours. Provided you have a significant block of working time that becomes routine and that your family, friends and clients are able to tune into, you can take advantage of the flexibility that working from home offers to improve your lifestyle.

Balance also features in the way you structure your working hours to ensure you get the best out of yourself and give adequate attention to the different aspects of your work. You need to focus not only on those core activities that bring in the money, but on the maintenance tasks too: those routine jobs that keep you functioning properly – staying informed, dealing with correspondence and organising your workspace.

In a traditional work setting, there are likely to be others whose specialist roles support your own. Chances are that when you are working from home it's all down to you. As well as fulfilling your main role, you may find that you are acting as your own office manager, PA, bookkeeper, marketing executive and odd job person. It may be impracticable or uneconomic to employ others in these capacities, and so you need to find ways by which the full range of activity required for success will be achieved. Rather than allowing tasks to build up until you are forced to have a bookkeeping splurge or a filing blitz, generate a varied work schedule to instil painless habits by weaving the different roles into your daily or weekly routine. Ask yourself the following questions:

- What are the various roles I need to fulfil? (List them.)
- Roughly what proportion of my time will be taken up by each of these?
- How does the market rate for these roles compare with the price per hour that I would put on my time in my main role?

When you are clear about the answers, you might like to consider a formal working arrangement to ensure the necessary services are fulfilled. If, for example, you decide that two hours a week is necessary for bookkeeping you might regard yourself as under contract to provide that service for one hour every Tuesday and Thursday, and approach the duty in just the same frame of mind as if you had been externally hired to fulfil the role. Similarly, you might act as a general administrator for half an hour every day. Visualising your different roles in this way can help you get to grips with them all and prevent some from being undervalued or overlooked. Putting a price on the various roles helps you get a handle on those tasks that it might make sense to contract out.

Focus

Who reminds you about things that need to be done? Who keeps your motivation high and helps out when you hit a tricky work problem? It's probably all down to you once again. But time and workload organisation can help make up for the absence of colleagues and mentors:

- It's even more important when you are working on your own to plan your activities over different time frames, to set clear, manageable challenges and to break down long-term projects into smaller chunks. It makes tasks easier to handle and gives you that much needed sense of progress.
- Stay on top of your schedule by whatever means suits you – paper-based or electronic – but stick to one simple system.

- Consider using checklists of daily and weekly routine tasks so that nothing gets missed.
- Break up your week with activities that involve human contact, and take steps to build and maintain your networks. Isolation is a frequent problem for those working from home. Other people similarly engaged can provide much needed advice and support.

Appropriate workspace

Attention to good organisation of your workspace can give a significant boost to productivity. The idea of firing off e-mails from the comfort of your bed or mapping out your business plan on a sun-drenched patio may be attractive and, indeed, there may be tasks that you can fulfil comfortably and effectively in unconventional settings, but the likelihood is that for a significant portion of your work, some form of office space is a must. Your home office does not have to be grand – forget those extravagant Sunday supplement conversions – but it should be comfortable and functional with attention paid to a layout that suits your working needs. Too often we neglect, in our home working arrangements, features that we would regard as essential if we were working elsewhere. We give ourselves insufficient or inappropriate space, and use the furniture and equipment that is to hand rather than spending a small amount of time and money creating a working environment that meets our requirements. Take account of the recommendations in Chapter 6 and consider the following fundamental elements:

- **A door you can close when necessary.**
Working on the dining room table may be convenient, but it presents a packing-up task every time you finish work for the day, and may also render you more open to interruption if other household members are present. Perhaps most importantly, it increases the difficulty of separating working life and home life.

- **A well-proportioned and adjustable chair.**

Often neglected, this is probably the most important investment you will make.

- **A work surface that is sufficiently spacious to accommodate essential equipment and gives you plenty of free space.**

It doesn't have to be a fancy desk; there are plenty of inexpensive, well-designed models available, and even foldaway options that could be considered if you are working in a multi-function area.

- **A pleasant, well-lit and comfortable environment.**

Working in a dingy boxroom, surrounded by piles of junk, has an effect on your work after a while.

- **Adequate storage equipment.**

If space is at a premium, go upwards rather than outwards. Shelves and stackable boxes may make up for a shortage of floor space.

There will be other factors to consider, depending on the nature of your work. If it involves clients visiting you, what sort of space do you have to receive them, and are there any local business restrictions or covenants that could lead to difficulty? If a great deal of your work is done on the telephone, do callers always receive a professional response, and might it be worth installing a second line with separate voicemail facilities? A second line can also be a valuable way of ensuring that work and leisure do not overlap. Set the work line to receive voicemail during your leisure time and do the same with the home line during your working hours.

There are other issues – legal, fiscal, regulatory – that may come into play with home working arrangements, particularly if your activities involve the employment of others, premises modification or the setting up of a space to be wholly and exclusively used as an office. But such matters are beyond the scope of this book. There are numerous other books and internet sites offering useful information and advice. Whatever the nature of your home-based work, take the trouble to clarify your needs, research any areas of uncertainty and organise yourself accordingly.

Organising yourself away from the office

If your work takes you regularly out on the road, you will be familiar with the organisational challenges such activity presents. For you it is a matter of keeping on top of your schedule, maintaining effective communication with your base, and ensuring that information you need is to hand and that equipment does not let you down. You share some of the challenges of balance and focus that are faced by those working from home. However, this section is directed not so much at those who are regularly on the road and are accustomed to the demands of mobile working as at the rest of us, for whom a trip away from the office is a more occasional event and one that may signal major disruption.

Business trips and conferences can put a large spanner in your personal organisation works. In the hours prior to your departure, you find yourself scurrying around to complete tasks that won't wait until your return. You finally manage to get away, drained and ratty, only to discover when you get to your destination that you have left a vital document behind. In the course of your trip you are pestered by messages relating to a minor crisis, resolution of which is dependent on a piece of information that lurks somewhere in your filing system. Finally, you arrive back, exhausted, burdened with new work and facing a backlog of correspondence, voicemail and e-mail messages.

The key to retaining your equilibrium, when work takes you away from the office for days at a time, is good planning and adherence, wherever possible, to normal routines.

Planning

- **Build some space into your schedule.**

  Scale back on any non-urgent work in the couple of days prior to your departure so that you can concentrate on those tasks that have to be completed before your return. Always allow more time for this than you think you will need.

- **Cover your home base.**

  Ensure that you have somebody who can check your mail, handle any minor crises, and find their way around your filing system and the information on your computer. Make sure you leave accurate contact numbers.

- **Check and double-check that you have everything you** *need* **for the trip.**

  Don't be tempted to take lots of paperwork in the vain hope that you will find time to deal with it. You are bound to come back with more than you took.

- **Put together an 'out of office kit'.**

  This should comprise of day-to-day accessories – envelopes, mini-stapler, pens, calculator, etc. Keep this handy so you can just drop it into your briefcase when you have a trip to make.

- **If you have a number of locations to visit, plan the order to minimise travelling time.**

  Journey-planning computer software may be of assistance in this.

- **Make sure that you know how to carry out any unfamiliar tasks.**

  These include picking up your voicemail messages remotely, picking up e-mail via the web or tapping into your organisation's network while on the road. Don't just trust to instructions from somebody else. Check the operation for yourself before you leave, to ensure it works. There is nothing worse than assuming that you will be able to stay in touch and then finding that you can't.

- **Most importantly, make sure that you have any**

passwords you need to access the above-mentioned facilities.

- **Change your voicemail message and set up e-mail auto-response so that callers know you are away and when you will be back.**

Include a mobile number if appropriate. Remember to change these messages when you return.

- **Check that you have everything you need installed on your laptop computer.**

For example, all relevant software, reference and contact material. The capacity and connectivity of today's portable computers means that you should be able to accommodate the same level of information as exists on your desktop PC.

- **If you are using public transport, earmark some tasks that are particularly appropriate for completion while travelling.**

Normally this will mean tasks that are not reliant on major paper shuffling, and can put up with some degree of interruption.

- **Don't underestimate the debilitating effect of travel.**

Allow some breathing space in your schedule before pitching into meetings and appointments.

- **If your trip involves foreign travel, check that you have all the adapters and rechargers you need to keep your equipment on the go.**

Make sure also that your mobile phone is set up to receive calls in the country or countries you are visiting.

- **If your laptop is set automatically to download updates to its operating system, security software or applications, you may want temporarily to disable this facility.**

It can be very frustrating, and potentially quite expensive, to find yourself in the middle of a lengthy download when you simply wish to check your e-mails during a brief stop at an airport or internet hotspot.

Maintaining routines

- **Resist the temptation to bundle up conference papers, 'to be sorted out when I get back'.**
  They will be destined to remain a disorganised bundle. Deal with any paperwork you receive while on the road in the same way as you would in the office (use the five Ds) and be particularly energetic with the 'discard' category.
- **Try to set some time aside during your day for dealing with routine correspondence and messages.**
  When you tap into your e-mail and voicemail, deal with as much of it as possible, rather than just scanning through for major problem messages. This way, you will greatly ease the backlog of work waiting for you on your return.
- **Set up a working area in your hotel room that is as conducive to productivity as possible.**
- **Keep track of expenses as you go.**
  It's much easier than trying to remember them afterwards.
- **Give yourself a break.**
  On conferences and business trips you can find yourself talking shop from breakfast until late evening. Build in some rest and relaxation if you don't want to return frazzled and exhausted.
- **Plan your first day back in the office before you return, but don't try to fit in too much.**

Summary

When working from home, you should ensure:

- **a balance between work and leisure;**
- **a balanced approach to the varied roles you may need to fulfil;**
- **attention to maintaining focus;**
- **good work space organisation.**

Operating away from your normal base requires effective planning to counteract the absence of facilities you normally take for granted, and maintenance of good work routines.

10

Keep up the good work

We are all familiar with the phenomenon of resolution fatigue. Good intentions launched with enthusiasm and vigour on 31 December are abandoned and forgotten by 10 January. It's no different with decisions to improve personal organisation. Reading this book is a start, but it won't bring all the results you want without some effort on your part.

Review your objectives

In Chapter 1 I invited you to set some objectives in respect of better personal organisation. No doubt you will have made progress with these as you have worked your way through the book, and hopefully too you will have gained new ideas on how you might tackle the organisational weaknesses you identified at the outset. It's now time to take stock. I would like to suggest that you review and refine your objectives, adjusting your priorities where necessary and setting target dates as required. Go back to the list you drew up in Chapter 1 and ask yourself the following three questions:

1. Which of these items, if any, have already been fully achieved? (Cross them off.)
2. What amendments do I wish to make to the remainder as a result of reading this book?
3. Are there areas of concern that I did not originally identify, but that I now realise require my attention?

Look at your amended list and prioritise the items on it A or B according to your estimate of their value in lifting your current level of personal organisation. The priority A items are the most important, the ones to concentrate on first. Set yourself an action plan for them, breaking down each major objective into its constituent tasks together with target dates. If you're carrying out this exercise on paper, you may wish to use a simple table format such as the one shown in Figure 10.1 to assist in drafting your proposals. When you're happy with your action plan, enter tasks and dates into whatever time-tracking system you are using, and get cracking with implementation. Don't take on too much at once. Remember that you need to give new habits time to become established.

Action plan

Main objective:

Target date:

Sub-goals and tasks	Start date	Target date

Figure 10.1   Action plan

Check your progress

Review progress regularly, weekly if possible, but not less than monthly. Give yourself immediate positive reinforcement or reward for every step forward, and use your successes as stepping stones to further achievement. Be kind with yourself when you have failed to achieve the progress you anticipated. Look for the reasons: perhaps you were trying to achieve too many things at once, maybe you didn't bash away for long enough to establish a new habit. Don't let yourself be lured into abandoning your goals, however. Reframe them and move on.

Visualise the way that you will work and the benefits that will accrue when you have perfected the new skills and ways of working. Visualisation is a very powerful means of seeing you through the short-term pain and into the long-term gain. Once your priority A objectives are well underway, you can move on to priority B.

Find ways of staying on track

Be on the lookout for any means by which you can keep your objectives at the front of your consciousness and your motivation high. For example, you might find it useful to adopt a weekly points system that rewards or penalises you for aspects of good or bad organisation. Points might be awarded along the following lines:

- **+10 points for every day planned in advance;**
- **−10 points for every 'to do' item carried over for more than one day;**
- **−10 points for every task performed that could have been delegated;**
- **+10 points for an empty filing tray at the end of the week;**
- **−2 points for every item in your filing tray in excess of 20 at the end of the week;**